The Language Complexity Game

The Language Complexity Game

Eric Sven Ristad

The MIT Press
Cambridge, Massachusetts
London, England

© 1993 Massachusetts Institute of Technology

All rights reserved. No part of this book may be reproduced in any form by any electronic or mechanical means (including photocopying, recording, or information storage and retrieval) without permission in writing from the publisher.

This book was set in Computer Modern by the author using LaTeX and was printed and bound in the United States of America.

Library of Congress Cataloging-in-Publication Data

Ristad, Eric Sven.
　The language complexity game / Eric Sven Ristad.
　　　p.　　cm. — (Artificial intelligence)
　Includes bibliographical references and index.
　ISBN 0-262-18147-9
　1. Natural language processing (Computer science)　2. Computational complexity.　I. Title.　II. Series: Artificial intelligence (Cambridge, Mass.)
QA76.9.N38R57 1993
401—dc20　　　　　　　　　　　　　　　　　　　　　　92-38731
　　　　　　　　　　　　　　　　　　　　　　　　　　　　CIP

Cover Art.
Unstable Equilibrium by Paul Klee, 1922.
34.5:17.8cm; watercolor over pencil on paper.
Copyright VG Bild-Kunst, Bonn.
In the collection of Paul Klee Foundation, Museum of Fine Arts, Bern.
Permission and print courtesy of Paul Klee Foundation.

To Suzanne Guerzon

Contents

	Foreword by Robert C. Berwick	ix
	Acknowledgments	xvii
1	**Introduction**	1
1.1	Prior Motivation	3
1.2	The Language Complexity Game	5
1.3	Summary of Results	8
	1.3.1 Interpretation of Human Language	9
	1.3.2 Complexity Thesis for Human Language	14
	1.3.3 Summary of Technical Results	16
2	**The Anaphora Problem**	21
2.1	Defining the Problem	23
2.2	Discussion	27
2.3	Summary of Anaphora Results	28
3	**Anaphoric Agreement**	31
3.1	The Standard Agreement Model	32
3.2	From Graph Coloring to Anaphoric Agreement	35
3.3	Agreement Reconsidered	36
	3.3.1 Theory of Paradigm Structure	40
	3.3.2 Paradigms for Anaphoric Elements	43
3.4	An Upper Bound on Anaphoric Uniqueness	45
4	**Referential Dependency**	49
4.1	The Referential Dependence Model	50
	4.1.1 Local c-command Configuration	51
	4.1.2 Control Configuration	55
	4.1.3 Strong Crossover Configuration	56
	4.1.4 Invisible Obviation Configuration	57
4.2	From Satisfiability to Referential Dependence	64

5	**Ellipsis**	73
5.1	Copy Model of Ellipsis	74
5.2	From QBF to Anaphoric Copying	79
5.3	Ellipsis Reconsidered	91
5.4	Function-Sharing Model of Ellipsis	94
5.5	An $\mathcal{NP}$ Algorithm for Anaphoric Sharing	102
6	**Implications of the Results**	109
6.1	Interpretation of Human Language	109
	6.1.1 The Study of Language	110
	6.1.2 The Parsing of E-Languages	117
6.2	The Complexity Thesis	120
6.3	The Language Complexity Game	124
	6.3.1 Methodological Suggestions	124
	6.3.2 Technical Contributions to Linguistics	128
A	**Background**	133
	Bibliography	139
	Index	145

Foreword by Robert C. Berwick

In his now-classic book on vision, David Marr opened with a simple question: What does it mean, to *see*? We open our eyes, and effortlessly, objects appear before us. The same holds for language. We open our mouths and unstop our ears, talk and listen, without apparent effort. Yet we know this surface simplicity is deceiving. Nearly four hundred years ago, the Cartesian rationalists realized that lurking beneath the seeming effortlessness of language lie mental computations of the subtlest sort. The eye is not a camera; the ear and mouth, neither tape recorders nor high fidelity speakers. As Descartes noted, we do not see cubes because the image of a cube is impressed into our brains like a key into wax; rather, elaborate mental computations build a *representation* of a cube in our heads. Similarly, the structure of sentences is assembled by our minds.

How then can language be both complex and subtle, yet simple and effortless? Ristad's book tackles this deepest of questions with all the power and precision of modern computer science, coming up with the best analysis of human language complexity since Chomsky's famous demonstration that natural languages cannot be described via simple linear patterns. His answer: human languages appear to be inherently computationally intractable, in a precise modern sense of intractable, *but* they verge just on the edge of intractability—as always, things could be worse. The results cover many parts of linguistics and different linguistic theories: morphophonology, metrical phonology, recent transformational grammar theories like Chomsky's *Barriers*, Generalized Phrase Structure Grammar. Indeed, the best part of Ristad's method is that it provides a theory-neutral stress test for all linguistic theories. It takes particular linguistic processes like agreement or ellipsis and shows that these processes *themselves* are intractable, no matter what the linguistic theory, thus bypassing endless quarrels about whose approach is "better." Ristad's research even shows how complexity analysis can do linguistics—for instance, how it can help choose between different theories of verb phrase ellipsis by diagnosing where a theory is too computationally complex and how it can be made simpler. So Ristad's work is not just for computational linguists, but for linguists too, pointing the way to a deeper marriage of linguistics and computation. Let us see how and why.

Until the middle of this century, one could not even ask such complexity questions about language precisely, because there was no apparatus to formally capture language's recursive nature, our ability to make "infinite use of finite means," in Wilhem von Humboldt's famous words. Then, in the early 1950s, Chomsky's invention of formal languages and his well-known complexity hierarchy of finite-state, context-free, and context-sensitive languages and their automaton counterparts opened the door to at least one way of attacking the problem. Chomsky showed that there was a deep sense in which *any* linguistic theory that tried to bottle all the complexity of language into simple linear patterns—finite-state automata—was doomed to failure. Roughly speaking, there is just not enough algebraic complexity in finite-state automata to be a match for the complexity of natural languages. Such linear pattern devices insist, for example, that sentences obey associativity: given three words a, b, and c, then for any finite-state automaton, a glued onto b and then c, abc, must be equivalent to (have the same meaning as, in all possible ways) as first gluing b and c together, and then gluing a onto the front of the bc combination. But this is surely inadequate, since there are English words and word sequences like *the dark blue sky* whose meaning depends upon the order in which its elements are put together: *the (dark blue sky)* surely means something different from *(the dark) blue sky*, but the purely linear "gluing" that finite-state automata provide cannot accommodate the alternative descriptions—a failure of "strong generative capacity" as Chomsky dubbed it. So human languages must be more complex than this.

Chomsky's demonstration proved pathbreaking in several ways. First, it showed how to formally measure the complexity of human language against the languages described by linguistic theories—what one might dub a *complexity mismatch metric*. If a theory cannot specify languages as complex as natural languages, then it does not measure up and can be tossed out on those grounds alone. If a theory's languages are as complex as those of human languages, then, so far so good. In other words, Chomsky's approach set a *lower bound* on the complexity of human languages—they had to be *at least* that complex. Moreover, the mismatch metric had the classic scientific virtue of *abstraction*: it avoided details irrelevant to the subject at hand. In particular, it was theory-neutral. No matter what the linguistic theory, no matter how that theory carved up its linguistic world into "syntax" or "semantics," the theory had to measure up. Third, the complexity mismatch analysis pointed the way to a solution: in the case of finite-state automata, the weakness in handling alternative, non-concatenative analyses tells us *what* must be made more powerful: we have to add hierarchical structure, phrases, to our theory of human languages.

If one can grasp what Chomsky did, then one already knows what Ristad's book is about. Ristad has updated Chomsky's complexity mismatch technique in two ways: first, by using our much deeper modern understanding of computation; and second, by applying that better understanding to the most current linguistic theories. Where Chomsky had to rely on automata as the way to classify a language's complexity, Ristad can arm himself with much better weaponry. Since the 1950s we have learned immensely more about computational complexity itself. In particular, we can now tote up *directly* how much time or space it takes to compute something, rather than go through the intervening step of looking at some mathematically constructed automaton that might or might not match up with the languages a theory specifies. Put another way, figuring out how complicated language is via the automaton route has alway been dangerously rough and roundabout, because it has never been clear anyway just why a formal mathematical object should mesh so neatly with some part of a biological product like language. Further, even when one pulls off the feat and ferrets out some part of some language that looks complicated—Chinese number names is a recent example—then one usually has only a lower bound on its complexity and so no handle on *how* complex it might really be at the top. Nor can we pick-and-choose the linguistic phenomenon we want to look at. Instead the game is to find some (usually out of the way) phenomenon that is hard, and that is that. What we really want is some way to corner a language's complexity from both the top and the bottom: to find out that language is at least so hard (with extraordinary luck, possible with the automaton approach), and to find out that it is at most so hard (almost surely impossible, since it demands an exact match of language to automaton). Finally, since the automaton approach focuses on just the sentences or sets of strings generated by a linguistic theory, it isn't really geared to peer inside to see what is complex about its *grammar*—the internal machinery or "I-language" in Chomsky's terminology that we are really interested in.

Ristad's new weapon, computational complexity theory, avoids all these pitfalls. First, it is abstracted in just the right way. Computational complexity theory looks at linguistic processes as *problems*. If one thinks about any linguistic process as a computational problem, for instance, in general determining the connections or referential dependencies in sentences like the link between *she* and *Elissa* in *Elissa thinks that Phil said that she was happy*, then the catch is that one could think of *many* algorithms and machine or brain implementations that might make this process hard or easy—suppose we used a parallel computer, for instance. Since we do not know much about the algorithms or implementation the brain uses, we need a method whose results remain invariant over all possible algorithms and implementations. This is just what computational complexity theory does. When it puts calculating referential dependencies in the *computational complexity class* of Nondeterministic Polynomial time ($\mathcal{NP}$), then as every computer scientist knows, that means that the linguistic problem itself is inherently hard, *no matter what* the linguistic theory, the algorithm, or machine/brain implementation.

Second, computational complexity theory explicitly takes grammars into account or not, as we choose, because the *input* to our problem statement can include the grammar explicitly or not. In other words, we can make the grammar a parameter of our problem or not. After that, it's our choice to see whether this inclusion makes sense depending on whether our problem formulation sheds light on linguistic structure. This immediately avoids common pitfalls that have appeared from time to time in automaton-driven complexity claims—for example, the notion that natural languages should be some subset of the context-free languages, because then that would explain how human languages are easily parsed (by people or machines, since we know of fast algorithms for parsing any context-free language). Whether true or not, such claims are bound to exclude grammars from their complexity calculations, because they can only look at *languages*, the external skin that grammars generate. In the only-context-free-languages case, since grammars are ignored, we do not get for free an explanation of why human language is easy to parse, because parsing languages means counting the grammars in, not out, since grammar size matters. (Whether human languages are in fact easy to parse or not is a separate empirical matter of course.) Computational complexity theory at least gives us the choice of including the grammar in our calculations.

Then too, computational complexity theory lets us *pick* what linguistic phenomenon we want to measure, instead of us having to go search for one. Don't care about exotica like Chinese number names? Then go after something more basic, like elliptical expressions (*Sue ate pizza and John too*) or agreement and syntactic category ambiguity. This is what Ristad does. Additionally, one can use complexity bounds to diagnose where a linguistic theory is too complex and suggest repairs. That is, we can use complexity theory to do linguistics. To do this, one must take a bold step and claim that linguistic processes can be *no more complex* than some upper bound. Ristad is no stranger to bold moves like this. He proposes that all natural language processes have the character of $\mathcal{NP}$-*complete* problems—they are as hard as any $\mathcal{NP}$ problems, but no harder. What does this mean? $\mathcal{NP}$-complete problems are computationally intractable—unsolvable in a reasonable amount of time by any known algorithm or machine—but not *too* intractable: their solutions are hard to find but easy to check once found. As a simple example, consider the traveling salesperson problem: find the shortest route that covers a networked collection of cities so that none are bypassed. It is easy to check a solution (just compute how long our route is), but finding the solution essentially means exhaustively searching all the possible complete tours. Pronoun antecedence again provides a simple natural language example. It is easy to check a proposed solution that *she* is *Elissa* in the example above, but, in general, Ristad shows that it can be difficult to find a solution in the first place. If you don't believe that, just try to figure out the links between the different *him*s in Ristad's example sentences such as *Before Bill, Tom, and Jack were friends, he wanted him to introduce him to him.*

It is here where Ristad's real skill comes into play. One must find a family resemblance between the linguistic problem under the microscope and a known computationally difficult problem. That takes a certain flair for detecting abstract similarities and formalizing linguistic theories. In our pronoun example, the key insight is that the constraints on pronoun linking pattern like the famous problem of coloring a map with a limited palette so that no two countries with shared borders have the same color—the *k colorability problem*. This problem is known to be computationally intractable. How is it like the pronoun problem? Two pronouns that are too close can't refer to the same person: in *He introduced him...*, *he* and *him* can't be the same person; if the pronoun moves far enough away, as in *He said John introduced him* then *he* and *him* can refer to the same person. So the syntactic domains form different country boundaries and possible pronoun antecedents are the different colors. Next Ristad shows that *any* k-colorability problem can be quickly transformed into a pronoun reference problem with the same solutions (if the original map was colorable with k colors, then the constructed pronoun reference problem has a valid linking of pronouns to antecedents). Since the problem of coloring an arbitrary map with k colors is known to be computationally intractable, then so must be the pronoun problem. Otherwise, we could quickly solve the map coloring problem by transforming it into a pronoun problem and solving *that* problem quickly, a contradiction.

Supposing now that linguistic processes are no harder than $\mathcal{NP}$, complexity theory restricts the class of adequate linguistic theories. On Ristad's assumptions, if a theory admits languages *more* complex than $\mathcal{NP}$, say theories that pose linguistic problems whose solutions are even hard to verify (such as those that are take so-called *Exponential Time*), then these theories are too complex. What's more, the particular linguistic problems leading to excessive complexity pinpoint the theory's weak points: one can focus on these linguistic phenomena to try to find a more constrained account of the same linguistic data. In particular, Ristad shows that this happens in an important area of linguistic research, elliptical constructions such as *John loves that person and Mary, him*.

To be sure, one can quibble about Ristad's tactics and assumptions. But this is true of all pioneering work. It is a simple exercise to find logical errors in Chomsky's seminal demonstration, for instance, but that does not detract from its importance. The bold step of setting an *upper* bound on the complexity of human languages may trouble some. Doesn't that have much the same flavor as saying that natural languages are only "mildly" context-sensitive, to cite another *au courant* approach? How do we know whether there is *any* limit to the complexity of natural languages? That's a valid criticism, but there are some differences. First, Ristad's method at least focuses on linguistic processes and grammars, not just on sentences as strings. Second, Ristad at least has an argument—however strong—about why we would expect human languages to have an $\mathcal{NP}$ nature: easy solutions or "witnesses" solutions to linguistic problems like pronoun coreference must exist because speakers can construct them, even though they are hard for listeners to find. There's a third, practical, point, too: Ristad makes good use of his assumptions to find defects in full-fledged linguistic theories.

Whatever one thinks of the upper bound assumption, Ristad's pioneering effort still stands. If natural languages inherently contain $\mathcal{NP}$-hard processes, then every adequate linguistic theory must encompass them and all linguistic theories are in the same complexity boat. That's a powerful result that completes the circle of analysis that we started in 1981 and reported on in our earlier study of the complexity of natural languages (Barton, Berwick, and Ristad, *Computational Complexity and Natural Language*, MIT Press 1987). There we applied computational complexity theory to a whole slew of then-current linguistic theories such as generalized phrase structure grammar, lexical-functional grammar, and two-level morphological analysis, but, as befits what we dubbed a progress report, we left behind a promissory note to tackle modern transformational theories. Ristad has kept that promise and more, proving directly that current transformational approaches like Chomsky's *Barriers* theory contain the seeds of computational intractability at their very core.

Only time will tell whether this second formal revolution in linguistics, the computational complexity revolution, will prove as lasting and influential as Chomsky's first. But if anything can make it last and influence linguistic science, it is this book.

Acknowledgments

This monograph would not exist without the love and kindness that Suzanne Guerzon provided me. The ideas in this monograph would not exist without the support and intellectual company of Robert C. Berwick, Noam Chomsky, Morris Halle, James Higginbotham, Howard Lasnik, Alec Marantz, Jorma Rissanan, and Edwin Williams.

A special thank you to Peter Elias, Eric Grimson, S. Jay Keyser, Albert Meyer, Michael Sipser, and Patrick Winston for their special help at MIT, and to Su-Shing Chen, Ken Steiglitz, and Robert Tarjan for theirs at Princeton.

For their invaluable assistance over the past five years, thanks to Stephen Anderson, Maggie Browning, Ezra Black, Jordan Cohen, Piroshka Csuri, Viviane Deprez, Teresa Ehling, Sandiway Fong, Faith Frick, Bob Freidin, Alessandra Giorgi, Shafi Goldwasser, Ken Hale, Gil Harman, Norbert Hornstein, William Idsardi, Michael Kenstowicz, Dave Kirsh, Andras Kornai, Glenn Kramer, Richard Larson, Tomás Lozano-Pérez, Scott Meredith, George Miller, Rolf Noyer, David Pesetsky, Geoff Pullum, Tanya Reinhart, Giorgio Satta, Barry Schein, Dafna Scheinwald, Peter Sells, Esther Torrego, Amy Weinberg, and Ken Wexler.

Thank you to the Paul Klee Foundation (Bern, Switzerland) for their kind permission to grace the cover with Paul Klee's "Unstable Equilibrium" (1922). This abstract symbolic work beautifully expresses the complexities of human language in a visual form.

The research reported in the monograph was supported primarily by Princeton University. In addition, the author gratefully acknowledges National Science Foundation Young Investigator Award IRI-9258517, and the support of Satish Rao and the NEC Research Institute, who made it possible for the author to complete this monograph in the summer of 1992. Although the results reported in the monograph were obtained since the author moved to Princeton, this monograph has its beginnings in the author's doctoral research at MIT. That research was supported by a generous IBM graduate fellowship to the author, by NSF Grant DCR-85552543 to R.C. Berwick (the author's thesis advisor), and by ONR contract N00014-85-K-0124 to the MIT Artificial Intelligence Laboratory.

The Language Complexity Game

1 Introduction

Human language is produced, comprehended, and acquired. Each of these cognitive activities is a process, a mapping from inputs to outputs. In language production, the input includes the intention to communicate a particular meaning, and the corresponding output is a linguistic representation of that meaning, which contains explicit instructions to the motor system on how to create an acoustic or visual signal that expresses the input meaning. In language comprehension, the input includes a sensation arising from such an acoustic or visual signal, and the corresponding output is a representation of the linguistic information in that sensation. If the sensation has linguistic significance (that is, it is assigned a linguistic representation), then the output representation will be used to reconstruct the intended meaning of the physical signal. In language acquisition, the input is evidence about a target human language, and the corresponding output is a hypothesis about the target human language.

In short, the language user is continually performing certain computations, called *language computations*, that produce and comprehend linguistic utterances and acquire new languages on exposure to linguistic evidence. The input to a language computation includes all information that affects the output of the computation. The output of acquisition is a hypothesis about the target language, and the output of comprehension or production is a linguistic representation. These computations are without question a central aspect of human language in need of scientific explanation. We therefore propose to study human language as a computational system.

A computational system employs a fixed, finite set of simple local operations to execute a (potentially infinite) class of computations. Each such computation is a sequence of discrete state transitions that maps a particular input to its corresponding output. A computational system may be described at various levels of abstraction: as sequences of state transitions (least abstract), as an algorithm (more abstract), or as a computational problem (most abstract). The sequence of state transitions specifies in the greatest detail exactly how a particular input is mapped into its corresponding output by a given computing machine. An algorithm specifies the allowable state transitions — how each state is mapped into its immediate successor by a computational system — and thereby constitutes a finite description of a (potentially infinite) set of state transition sequences. A computational problem specifies only the relation between the inputs and outputs of the computation, abstracting away from all issues of how that relation is to be calculated by a computing machine.

Computations consume abstract resources, such as time and space. Time corresponds to the number of state transitions used to map a given input into its corresponding output, while space corresponds to the maximal amount of information in an intermediate state in the state transition sequence. The structure of a computation is strongly related to the amount of time and space it requires. In general, more complex or powerful mappings require more time and space to compute. Not only does the problem statement abstract away from many unimportant details of a computation, but it does so in a way that preserves the essential structure of the computation, including its resource requirements.

The first step in our research program is to characterize the three central computations of human language (comprehension, production, and acquisition) at the highest level of abstraction, as computational problems. It is difficult to describe language computations in an empirically-motivated manner. However, it profits our understanding of language to do so, because each such description is, in effect, a computational theory of a portion of language. Our computational theory must be framed abstractly, in terms of computational problems, simply because the empirical evidence available today cannot possibly justify a more detailed description of these mental computations. The aggregation of all such problem statements is a complete computational theory of human language, at the highest level of abstraction.

The second step in our research program is to determine the rate at which language computations consume the abstract resources of time and space. We will accomplish this by analyzing the computational complexity of our language problems. Complexity analysis will help us better understand the structure of language computations, in part because the complexity of a computational problem is inherited by less abstract descriptions of the same computation. Complexity analysis will relate language computations to other computations whose structure we understand. And complexity results will provide a design target for language algorithms, which is the next step of our research program.

In short, the two most fundamental questions we can ask about a language computation are: what is the relation between the inputs and outputs of that computation, and what computational resources are required to calculate that relation? The answer to the first question is a computational theory of human language. The answer to the second question is an understanding of the structure of that computation.

To study human language as we have proposed here is not to say that language is designed for efficient computation, or even that language is based on a general-purpose digital computer. Nor do we claim that language is designed for communication or that its primary use is to communicate when we view human language from an information-theoretic perspective. The goal of this research is to understand human language in its own terms. We believe that important aspects of human language receive an insightful interpretation in terms of computation and information.

This introductory chapter consists of three sections. Section 1.1 motivates the computational study of human language. Section 1.2 sets forth our research methodology as an adversarial game between two players, the first of which attempts to establish that language is more complex than previously thought, and the second who tries to establish that language is less complex than previously thought. The outcome of this language complexity game is a precise computational theory of language, that is empirically correct in all computationally significant respects. Section 1.3 summarizes the three central results of our research: (i) a conceptually and technically coherent interpretation of human language, (ii) a strong complexity thesis for human language, and (iii) precise, empirically-motivated definitions for a related set of language problems, with tight complexity bounds (that is, several rounds of the language complexity game).

We return to related issues in chapter 6, where we discus the implications of our results for the study of language as a whole, with particular consideration of the disciplines of generative linguistics, computational linguistics, and psycholinguistics. We also evaluate the significance of classifying the computational complexity of a biological information-processing system.

1.1 Prior Motivation

The research described herein is motivated solely by the desire to improve our understanding of human language. If it succeeds in that, then it succeeds; if it fails in that, then it fails.

We may also ask what motivated us to attempt a computational study of human language in the first place, and why our investigation took the form that it did. Why did we believe that a computational approach would advance our understanding of human language? And what motivated us to establish a complexity thesis for human language?

The history of language research is one of gross complexity mismatches, where competing theories of language have either been absurdly powerful or laughably weak. Markov models and finite state machines (linear time and constant space) have been promoted as descriptively-adequate models of all aspects of human language, as have unrestricted rewriting systems (unbounded time and space). This discrepancy has not significantly narrowed in recent years.[1] Current research methodology in theoretical linguistics, psycholinguistics, and computational linguistics is likely produce more such complexity mismatches, for two reasons. On the one hand, the pressure to elegantly describe complex linguistic phenomenon requires models of language with powerful primitives and powerful means of combining them. This, of course, leads to overly powerful theories. On the other hand, the prevailing assumption among language researchers that language computations are trivial leads to trivial models (particularly when in conjunction with a behaviorist perspective on language). Such extreme disagreement on such a central computational issue could only arise because the computations of human language have not hitherto been the subject of serious investigation.

---

[1] Let us briefly consider a recent example of a complexity mismatch. In the early 1980s, generalized phrase structure grammar (GPSG) was proposed by Gazdar [32] as a plausible theory of human language, based on ideas due to Harman [38], with the special merit of providing "the beginnings of an explanation for the obvious, but largely ignored, fact that humans process the utterances they hear very rapidly." [32, p.155] In the original formulation of [32], the problem of deciding whether a given string was generated by a given GPSG is undecidable [80, 101]. In a later, more careful and more comprehensive formulation [33], the recognition problem for GPSGs required at least exponential time [84]. In roughly the same period of time, a class of bounded-context pushdown-stack parsers initially proposed by Marcus [68] were widely touted as a plausible theory of human linguistic performance [6, 7, 8, 20, 110]. In Marcus' original formulation, these parsers required at most time linear in the size of their input [8, p.192]. In a more powerful "cascaded" formulation due to Berwick and Weinberg [8], at most quadratic time was required. There is a vast discrepancy between an undecidability lower bound for GPSG and a linear time upper bound for the bounded-context parsers. The discrepancy does not narrow significantly in later formulations: the gap between an exponential time lower bound and a quadratic time upper bound remains almost incomprehensibly large, especially when we consider that both are allegedly plausible theories of human language, and that both attempt to provide accounts of roughly the same linguistic phenomena.

We propose to redress this deficiency by developing a complexity thesis for human language that provides tight upper and lower bounds on the computational complexity of human language. Our complexity thesis states that language computations are complete for nondeterministic polynomial time (NP-complete). In the body of this monograph, we defend this complexity thesis with mathematical proofs that rely only on the empirical facts of linguistic knowledge, and on the uncontroverted assumption that these facts generalize in a reasonable manner. For this reason, these complexity results apply to all adequate theories of linguistic knowledge. Our complexity thesis strengthens Chomsky's early work on the mathematics of language [14], with the advantages of a better understanding of language and a more precise theory of structural complexity.[2]

Next, we outline a research methodology called the language complexity game, whose expected outcome is an accurate understanding of the structure and complexity of language computations.

1.2 The Language Complexity Game

How can we avoid a complexity mismatch in our own research? In order to ensure the accuracy of our complexity thesis, we will play the following two-player adversarial game, called the *language complexity game*. The idea of this game is that two abstract players will take turns trying to improve our understanding of human language computations. One of the players (the maximizer) will attempt to establish that language computations are more complex than previously thought, while the other player (the minimizer) will attempt to establish that that language computations are less complex than previously thought. At any given point, either player may start a new game by proposing a plausible model of a new class of linguistic knowledge. The game terminates when neither player is able to improve the current understanding of human language in a way that significantly affects its computational complexity. The last player to improve the current understanding (that is, take a turn in the game) wins. The more accurate a language model is, the more

---

[2]Our better understanding of language is the result of more than three decades of productive inquiry. Our technical results employ the mathematical theory of computational complexity, which is a more precise theory of structural complexity than the hierarchy of formal grammars/automata that was employed in [14].

difficult it is to improve on it. Therefore this rule encourages players to do their best to end the game with their current move, by proposing the most accurate language model that they are capable of. Both players share a common goal, to understand human language, and hence both players benefit from participating in the game although only one player is officially declared the winner.

In this monograph, we will play five rounds of the language complexity game in the domain of anaphora. This game is defined by the Anaphora Problem, which is the computational problem of determining the antecedents of the anaphoric elements in an utterance without introducing any new information. Our game begins in chapter 3 with the maximizer, who formalizes a widely-accepted model of anaphoric agreement and proves that the Anaphora Problem cannot be solved efficiently according to this model of agreement. The minimizer responds by demonstrating the empirical inadequacy of the agreement model, proposing an empirically-superior model of anaphoric agreement, and proving that the Anaphora Problem can be solved rather quickly according to this improved agreement model. The maximizer responds in chapter 4 by expanding the empirical scope of the game. He formalizes a sophisticated model of referential dependencies (based on disjoint reference conditions) and proves that the Anaphora Problem is computationally intractable according to this model of referential dependencies. The game continues in chapter 5.

The structure of the game should be clear from this example. Each language complexity game consists of a chosen domain, defined by a computational problem L solved by the language user in that domain. Each turn of the game consists of three components: (i) a constructive critique of the empirical inadequacy of the current language model M, (ii) a precise statement of an improved language model M', and (iii) a tight bound on the complexity the chosen language problem L with respect to the improved model M'. For the maximizer's turn to be valid, he must establish that his improved model M' is more complex (with respect to the chosen problem L) than the minimizer's model M; to do this, the maximizer must prove a tight lower bound on the complexity of M'. Likewise, for the minimizer's turn to be valid, he must establish that his improved model M' is less complex than the maximizer's model M, by proving a tight upper bound on the complexity of M'.

Each turn in this game advances our understanding of human language. The first component, a constructive critique of current wisdom, certainly improves our understanding of human language, almost by definition. By requiring the maximizer to propose a more complex language model and justify it empirically (the second component of each turn taken by the maximizer), we are likely to discover the complexities of language, which will enrich the domain of scientific discussion and ensure that our language models are not too simple. By requiring the minimizer to propose a less complex language model and justify it empirically, we ensure that our language models are only as powerful as is justified by linguistic phenomena. The third component, a tight complexity bound, consists of two parts: a complexity classification (a theorem) and a proof of that theorem. The complexity classification improves our understanding by placing the chosen language problem L in a well-understood hierarchy of computational complexity, where problems in the same complexity class share important structural properties. The complexity classification is either a lower bound (due to the maximizer) or an upper bound (due to the minimizer). Lower bounds are typically proven by a reduction from another, well-understood computational problem, while upper bounds are proven by exhibiting an algorithm to solve the language problem L. Reductions advance our understanding by revealing the sources of complexity in the current language model. These sources of complexity will in turn suggest research projects, whose goal is to justify or falsify each source of complexity with additional empirical evidence. Algorithms improve our understanding of language computations because an algorithm is a more detailed description of given computation than the corresponding problem statement.

Our confidence in the outcome of the language complexity game depends entirely on how well the game is played. If the game is played poorly, or with little desire to win on the part of either player, then the outcome of the game cannot be trusted. A masterful maximizer may easily fool a naive or ignorant minimizer into believing that language computations are more complex than they in fact are, and vice versa. Only if the game is played skillfully by competent players, with both players determined to win, can we have confidence in the game's outcome.

One such outcome of the language complexity game is upper and lower bounds on the computational complexity of human language. There can be no principled distinction between our confidence in upper bounds and our confidence in lower bounds, simply because both derive from our confidence in the language complexity game as a whole. If either player does not play well, then neither upper nor lower bounds can be trusted. The maximizer can just as easily mislead the minimizer as the minimizer can mislead the maximizer. For this reason, neither upper nor lower bound is intrinsically stronger than the other, earlier claims to the contrary [85].

To summarize, each game is defined by a particular language problem, which is an abstract description of a class of language computations. The current state of a language complexity game consists of the current model for that language problem. The state of the "global" language complexity game, then, is the set of current language models. The complexity of this set is bounded below by the greatest lower bound in the set. In this monograph, we conduct a comprehensive language complexity game in the domain of anaphora. According to the quiescent state of this game and others [85], the complexity of human language computations is bounded below by NP-hardness, and above by inclusion in $\mathcal{NP}$. In section 1.3.2, we will recast this mathematical fact as a complexity thesis for human language.

1.3 Summary of Results

This monograph contains three major results, which we discuss in order below. First, we present a conceptually and technically coherent interpretation of human language, that improves on prior interpretations and frameworks. Second, we state and motivate our complexity thesis for human language, that the computations of human language are NP-complete. Third, we summarize our technical results. These consist of precise, empirically-plausible definitions for a representative set of language problems, with tight complexity bounds (that is, several rounds of the language complexity game).

In the final chapter of the monograph, chapter 6, we consider the implications of our complexity results for theories and models of human language. In that chapter, we explicitly compare our proposed framework for studying language to other linguistic frameworks, including generative linguistics, computational linguistics, and psycholinguistics.

1.3.1 Interpretation of Human Language

The first major result of this monograph is an interpretation of human language, a technical and conceptual framework within which to address substantive questions about language. It must answer the four conceptual questions: (i) what is a human language? (ii) what is language acquisition? (iii) what is language production? and (iv) what is language comprehension?

We interpret human language as follows. We model a particular human language (that is, an idiolect) as the set M of linguistic structures possible in that language. Each structure in M is a representation of some instance of linguistic knowledge. The set of humanly possible languages, the so-called *universal grammar*, is therefore the model class $\mathcal{M}$ of all humanly-possible languages. That is, $\mathcal{M}$ is a set containing all humanly-possible sets of linguistic representations.

We model language acquisition as a computation from a stream of evidence about a target human language to a hypothesis M about the target human language, $M \in \mathcal{M}$. We model language production as a computation f_M whose input is some extralinguistic information, including but not limited to the intention to communicate a particular meaning, and whose output is a linguistic representation r, $r \in M$, of that extralinguistic information in that language M. The output representation r will contain explicit instructions to the sensori-motor system on how to create an acoustic or visual signal that expresses the input meaning. We model language comprehension as a computation f_M whose input is some extralinguistic information, including but not limited to a sensation arising from such an acoustic or visual signal, and whose output is a representation r, $r \in M$, of the extralinguistic information in that language M. If the extralinguistic information includes a sensation with linguistic significance (that is, a sensation that is assigned a linguistic representation), then the output representation r will be used by other cognitive processes to reconstruct the intended meaning of the physical signal. Extralinguistic information includes intentions, sensations, beliefs, models of agents (other agents as well as oneself), mental lexicon, conceptual system, and so forth.

More generally, human language is a computation f whose input is extralinguistic information i and a set M of possible linguistic representations, and whose output is a particular linguistic representation r

of the information i in the language M, along with a revised language hypothesis M' (where $r \in M$, $M \in \mathcal{M}$, and $M' \in \mathcal{M}$). This unitary language computation is (1):

(1) $$f(i, M) = \langle r, M' \rangle$$

The function f and universal grammar $\mathcal{M}$ constitute the innate endowment of the language user. A particular human language is a stable set M of linguistic representations with the concomitant specialization of the language-universal function $f(\cdot, \cdot)$ to the language-particular function f_M, where $f_M(i) \doteq f(i, M)$.

A crucial feature of this interpretation that distinguishes it from widespread and unexamined belief is that there is no principled distinction between the comprehension and production of linguistic utterances. Comprehension and production are not inverses: both are the identical function f_M from the extralinguistic information provided by other cognitive processes to a linguistic representation of that information. The output of language comprehension is a linguistic representation, not a meaning. The output of language production is a linguistic representation, not a sound. Differences between comprehension and production — such as the fact that production typically involves the creation of a physical signal arising from motor activity under the conscious volition of the language user, whereas comprehension typically does not — are outside the purview of the human language, and therefore should not continue to distract the student of language, as they have for centuries.[3]

Another distinguishing feature of our interpretation is that language acquisition is crucially related to the comprehension and production of language. According to this view, which has its root in Cartesian linguistics, it is the repeated comprehension *and* production of language that allows the language learner to acquire a language.

Three caveats are in order.

As stated above, our proposed interpretation of language is nonconstructive, because it does not explain how such infinite objects as a

---

[3] As stressed by the great nineteenth century linguist Wilhelm von Humboldt, every sound uttered as language is assigned a complete meaning and linguistic representation in the mind of the producer: "The sentence is not to be constructed, is not to be gradually built up of components, but is to be expressed all at once in a form compressed to unity.... Man inwardly relates a complete meaning with every sound emitted as language: that is, for him it is a complete utterance. Man does not intentionally emit merely an isolated word, even though his statement according to our viewpoint may only contain such an entity." [102, pp.110–111]

particular language M or the universal grammar $\mathcal{M}$ are to be represented finitely in the language user. However, our interpretation is not inherently nonconstructive. For instance, we may straightforwardly add a "principles and parameters" component [18] to our interpretation as follows. The only change is that the universal grammar now includes a finite vector of finite-valued parameters $\vec{\theta} = \theta_1, \theta_2, \ldots, \theta_n$. Without loss of generality, we henceforth assume that these n parameters are binary-valued. Then the ith *parameter setting* $\rho_i(\vec{\theta})$ for the parameter vector $\vec{\theta}$ is the ith string in $\{0,1\}^n$, that assigns a value of either 0 or 1 to each parameter in $\vec{\theta}$. As before, we model each particular language as the set M of linguistic representations possible in that language. Universal grammar is a parameterized class $\mathcal{M}$ of such language models, that is, a function u from $\{0,1\}^n$ to M, that takes the ith parameter setting $\rho_i(\vec{\theta})$ to the ith model $u(\rho_i(\vec{\theta})) = M$, $M \in \mathcal{M}$.

For expository clarity and mathematical tractability, we have chosen to model human language as the discrete function f. Nothing hinges on the fact that this function f is discrete, deterministic, and without internal state. A more general formulation of f as a conditional probability distribution may be in order, where $f(r, M'|i, M)$ is the conditional probability that (i) the language hypothesis is revised to M' from M given extralinguistic information i and (ii) that linguistic representation r is assigned to extralinguistic information i in language M. We would model the naturalness (or so-called markedness) of languages by a prior distribution on the space of possible languages $\mathcal{M}$. Perhaps a distance measure on the space M of possible linguistic representations would also prove useful in characterizing the computable distribution f. Finally, we would require probabilistic models of other cognitive systems, which could be summarized in a distribution on the space of possible extralinguistic information.

Given the current state of our scientific understanding of language, it is not possible to plausibly describe any component of the proposed interpretation in a comprehensive manner. We cannot plausibly describe the universal grammar $\mathcal{M}$, the universal language computation f, any particular language M in $\mathcal{M}$, or in fact any particular linguistic structure r in any particular language M.

In order to proceed with our investigation, we will decompose each model M into a set of disjoint "submodels." Each submodel will represent a natural class of linguistic knowledge, and each representation in that submodel will represent a natural class of linguistic knowledge about some linguistic and extralinguistic information. We must now include linguistic information as inputs to our language subcomputations, because we have broken each linguistic structure into a set of disjoint substructures, and substructures will in general depend on other substructures. Therefore we must now describe language comprehension and production for a given language submodel as a function from linguistic as well as extralinguistic information.

Consider, for example, the submodel of referential dependencies presented in chapter 2. This submodel represents the language user's knowledge of how anaphoric elements determine their reference. An *anaphoric element* is a linguistic element, such as a pronoun or reflexive, that does not have intrinsic reference. The *linguistic antecedent* of an anaphoric element is the linguistic element from which the anaphoric element obtains its reference. In the English utterance *John saw himself*, we would say that language users know that the reflexive element *himself* depends on the proper noun *John* for its reference: that the reflexive *himself* refers to whatever mental object the proper noun *John* refers to, as mediated by the mental lexicon. To represent this fact of the language user's linguistic knowledge, we will postulate a relation of antecedence between anaphoric elements (such as reflexives and pronouns) and their linguistic antecedents (such as proper nouns). A particular structure r in this submodel M of referential dependencies consists of an asymmetric, irreflexive, and transitive relation of antecedence from anaphoric elements to their linguistic antecedents (that is, from referentially-dependent elements to referentially-independent elements). The submodel M consists of all such relations possible in a given language. The submodel class $\mathcal{M}$ consists of all humanly-possible submodels of referential dependencies. In order to assign a representation r to some extralinguistic information i in this submodel, we crucially require certain linguistic information, such as information about the phrase structure assigned to i by other language submodels.

An important implication of our interpretation of human language is that communication between producer and comprehender will be successful only if there is sufficient overlap in their language models and they are receiving approximately the same extralinguistic information. For example, they must have roughly the same mental lexicon and conceptual system, they must have reasonably accurate models of each other and of the discourse, and they must be experiencing similar visual and aural sensations.

We have proposed an interpretation of language as a completely internalized cognitive system, more internalized that the I-language view of Chomsky [20]. In that and other work, Chomsky contrasts two views of human language, one of 'language in extension' (E-language) and the other of 'language in intention' (I-language). The E-language view holds that each particular human language is an infinite set of linguistic expressions [10], perhaps paired with their meanings [64], where each expression is a string of symbols, representing the words of a grammatical sentence. According to the I-language view, each particular language is a finite description of the infinite relation between the forms and meanings of expressions.[4] Another I-language view, that is arguably more faithful to the practice of generative linguistics, is that a particular language is a finite procedure that enumerates the infinite set of complete linguistic representations possible in that language.[5]

In the interpretation we have proposed, each particular human language is a finite computing machine that executes a computation from some extralinguistic information to a linguistic representation of that information. The translation of our proposal into historical terminology is misleading in certain important respects. For example, we would argue that the notion of an "expression" is incoherent. However, if compelled to press our ideas into historical molds, we might suggest that a particular language be viewed as a finite machine that performs a computation f whose input is (information about) the form and meaning of a linguistic expression and whose output is the linguistic representation of that form and meaning. The generative procedure of a particular language is a partial, extensional characterization of a subset of the possible outputs of the unitary language computation f.

In section 6.1.1, we contrast our interpretation of language with prior interpretations, including those due to Chomsky, Fodor, and Marr. Let us now consider our constructive complexity thesis for human language,

---

[4] "The generative grammar of a particular language (where 'generative' means nothing more than 'explicit') is a theory that is concerned with the form and meaning of expressions of this language." [20, p.3]

[5] ". . . a [particular] language is a particular generative procedure that assigns to every possible expression a representation of its form and its meaning . . . . The language, so construed, 'strongly generates' a set of structural descriptions; we may take this set to be the structure of the language." [21, p.5]

which states that language computations are NP-complete.

1.3.2 Complexity Thesis for Human Language

The second major result of this monograph is the thesis that language computations are NP-complete.[6] This complexity thesis is a substantive, falsifiable claim about human language that is directly supported by the quiescent state of the language complexity game.

The complexity thesis also has a certain intuitive appeal. According to our interpretation, language comprehension and language production are the same computational process, from the same inputs to the same outputs. Therefore, if the producer and comprehender have roughly the same extralinguistic information as input, they will output the same linguistic representation using the same computational resources of time and space. This suggests that language computations cannot be too complex. However, it is not always the case that the producer and comprehender have roughly the same extralinguistic information as input. In some cases, such as when their mental lexicons or conceptual systems differ significantly, their inputs will be so different that it is impossible in principle for them to output the same linguistic representation. In other cases, such as when the comprehender's sensory information is impoverished, their inputs will be sufficiently similar that it is possible in principle for them to output the same linguistic representation, although comprehension will require significantly more computational resources than production did. In short, our interpretation suggests that language computations can be complex, but not too complex.

This is exactly the structure of an NP-complete problem. An NP-complete problem is difficult to solve because although its input contains all the information needed to uniquely determine the output, the information need not be in a computationally accessible form, and so an intractable amount of calculation may be required to extract that crucial information from the input. However, an NP-complete problem is not too difficult to solve, because once the appropriate information (the so-called "efficient witness") has been obtained from the input, it

---

[6]The upper and lower bounds of our proposed complexity thesis are tight enough to tell us exactly where the adequate linguistic theories are, not only where they are not. This is in contrast to Chomsky's 1956 complexity thesis [14], which is not as useful because — as argued by Chomsky [15] — the upper bound is very loose, the lower bound is weak, and the formal language theory of structural complexity is not sufficiently precise.

is easily verified to be correct.

It is the task of comprehension to find the intended representation, given extralinguistic information (including the sensation of the utterance) as input. When the input information is impoverished or inaccurate or the utterance is missing crucial disambiguating information, and there are global dependencies in the linguistic representation, then the task of finding the intended output representation quickly becomes very difficult. Yet we know comprehension cannot be too difficult, simply because there is always an efficient witness, namely the linguistic representation from which the utterance was produced. If only the comprehender had the same extralinguistic information that the producer did, then he would be able to efficiently compute the intended linguistic representation of the utterance, simply because the producer did. A related implication is that the cooperative interaction between the producer and comprehender is crucial to overcoming the computational intractability inherent in language comprehension and production.

The central consequence of this complexity thesis for human language is that empirically adequate models (and theories) of language will give rise to NP-completeness, under an appropriate idealization to unbounded inputs (see [85, appendix A.2]). If a language model is more complex than $\mathcal{NP}$, say PSPACE-hard, then our complexity thesis predicts that the system is unnaturally powerful, perhaps because it overgeneralizes from the empirical evidence or misanalyzes some linguistic phenomena.[7] Such a language model must be capable of describing unnatural or impossible human languages. If, however, a complete language model is less complex than NP-hard, then it is predicted to be unnaturally weak, most likely because it does not adequately account for some complex linguistic phenomena. Such a model will not be able to describe certain important facts about human languages. Otherwise the language model is NP-complete and is potentially adequate, pending the outcome of more exacting tests of scientific adequacy.

The complexity thesis also makes predictions for human linguistic performance, although its predictions in this domain are extremely weak, virtually impossible to falsify, and therefore largely uninteresting. The complexity thesis predicts that there is some finite input size k such

---

[7]Without loss of correctness, we assume for the purposes of exposition that $\mathcal{P} \neq \mathcal{NP}$, although none of the substantive claims in this monograph hinge on this assumption.

that as the size n of the input grows beyond that fixed size k, the rate at which computational resources are consumed by human language computations is bounded above by a certain function $f(n)$ in the size n of the input, in the worst case. These issues are discussed in some depth in [4, 8, 9]. Such predictions are most definitely *not* the point of this work, and we will not dwell on them.

In short, our complexity thesis is an independent guide to the study of language. It is useful because it is a simple decision procedure with which to evaluate language models, both theoretical and implemented. The student of language will find it helpful, because, as this monograph demonstrates, language models that have complexity outside of $\mathcal{NP}$ are ripe for reanalysis. And as should be clear from this discussion, NP-completeness is not the stigma that many apparently think it is. In fact, exactly the opposite is true. Our complexity thesis argues that less complex models of language are fundamentally inadequate (barring, of course, a revolution in our understanding of language or of nondeterminism).

1.3.3 Summary of Technical Results

The technical content of this monograph is apportioned into four chapters. The reader is referred to the lone appendix, appendix A, to review the technical background necessary to appreciate the mathematics of our investigation. There we review the theory of computational complexity and define the computational problems referred to throughout the monograph.

Language Complexity Game for Anaphora. We begin our language complexity game in chapter 2 with the computational problem of determining the intended antecedents of the anaphoric elements in a discourse (the Anaphora Problem). The language models in this game are all based on empirical facts of the language user's conscious knowledge of anaphoric reference, for example, that the utterance *Mary said John saw him* cannot mean 'Mary said John saw John' or 'Mary said John saw Mary' (two cases of disjoint reference) and that the utterance *John saw himself* must mean 'John saw John' (a case of obligatory coreference). The language complexity game for anaphora consists of five turns, spread out over three chapters.

The maximizer begins in chapter 3 by formalizing a model of anaphoric agreement based on the widely-accepted idea that an anaphoric element and its antecedent cannot disagree in certain respects, such as gender, animacy, and number. The Anaphora Problem is shown to be NP-hard in the maximizer's model of anaphoric agreement. The minimizer replies by demonstrating the inadequacy of the standard view of anaphoric agreement, and proposing an improved model of anaphoric agreement, called the anaphoric equivalence condition. The Anaphora Problem is shown to be in $\mathcal{P}$ in the minimizer's model of anaphoric agreement.

On the third turn, which constitutes chapter 4, the maximizer expands the scope of the game to include certain disjoint reference phenomenon, for example, the fact that in the utterance *He saw him* the two pronouns *he* and *him* are understood as having disjoint reference. The maximizer proposes a model of referential dependencies based on these disjoint reference facts, and proves that the Anaphora Problem is NP-hard in this model of referential dependencies.

The game continues in chapter 5, where the maximizer once again expands the scope of the anaphora complexity game to include certain facts about ellipsis, for example, the fact that the utterance *Max hates his neighbors and so does Sam* is ambiguous between two interpretations, that may be paraphrased as 'Max and Sam both hate Max's neighbors' and 'Max and Sam each hate their own neighbors'. The maximizer formalizes a model of ellipsis based on a widely-accepted linguistic theory, and proves that the Anaphora Problem is PSPACE-hard according to this model of ellipsis. On the fifth turn, the minimizer replies by falsifying the maximizer's model of ellipsis, sketching an improved model of ellipsis, and then proving that the Anaphora Problem is inside $\mathcal{NP}$ according to the improved model of ellipsis.

When these five turns are accounted for, the final state of the language complexity game for anaphora is a precise, empirically-motivated description of language computations involving anaphora. We may have confidence in this description, because it is the outcome of several rounds an aggressively-played adversarial game, where one player has attempted to prove the Anaphora Problem as complex as possible, and the other player has attempted to prove the Anaphora Problem as simple as possible. An incidental outcome of this language complexity game is a tight upper and lower bound on the computational complexity of anaphora. The complexity of the Anaphora Problem is bounded above by inclusion in $\mathcal{NP}$ and below by NP-hardness.

Companion Results. Although the language complexity game of this monograph is, in our opinion, the strongest language complexity game played to date, it is not the first. We are aware of two other language complexity games. One is for phonological and morphological computations, and the other for morpho-syntactic computations.

The language complexity game for phonology and morphology turns primarily on the phonological representation problem (roughly, the computational problem of assigning a permissible phonological representation to a sequence of phonemes or to a morpho-syntactic representation), and secondarily on a subproblem of acquisition (roughly, to determine whether a hypothesized morpho-phonological model is consistent with the acquisition evidence). The language models in this game are all based on the language user's knowledge of what is a possible sequence of linguistic sounds in his language and how to articulate such sound sequences. Approximately seven turns in this ongoing game have been played to completion.

The maximizer began the first turn in the language complexity game for phonology in 1968 by proposing a comprehensive model of phonological dependencies, called the segmental model [23]. The comprehension, production and acquisition problems for the segmental model were all shown to be undecidable and to remain PSPACE-hard under severe restrictions [83]. The minimizer [87] replied by proposing a simplified segmental model capable of representing all known phonological dependencies and then proving that the phonological representation problem for this model is in $\mathcal{NP}$. On the third turn, the maximizer [87] concludes this game for segmental phonology by establishing the NP-hardness of the phonological representation problem in the simplified segmental model.

Although the outcome of this game is a significantly improved segmental model, the simplified segmental model is still capable of representing extremely unnatural or impossible phonological dependencies as well as natural dependencies. To overcome this difficulty, in [83, 86, 88], the players agree to restrict the domain of discussion to the most natural class of phonological dependencies, called assimilation. The maximizer takes the first turn in this game, by formalizing a phonological model based on prominent ideas in modern phonology (the so-called autosegmental or nonlinear theories of phonology), and then proving that the comprehension problem for this autosegmental model is NP-hard. The minimizer replies by establishing its inclusion in $\mathcal{NP}$. Next, the maximizer expands the domain of discussion to include the relation between the morphology and phonology of words. He formalizes a model of the morpho-phonology based on the theory of prosodic morphology, and proves that two subproblems of comprehension and acquisition are NP-hard according to this model. The minimizer concludes the game by establishing their inclusion in $\mathcal{NP}$.

A second companion language complexity game is defined by the computational problem of assigning a syntactic structure to a sequence of ambiguous words (the Lexical Resolution Problem).[8] The language models in this game all relate to the language user's knowledge of syntactic agreement, for example, that the subject and verb must agree on number in the sentences *The boat floats* and *The boats float*. The models are also able to represent the ambiguity of words, for example, that the word *buffalo* can be either a verb ('to bewilder') or singular or plural noun with multiple meanings (including 'wild oxen', 'buffalofish', or 'Buffalo, NY'). The language complexity game for the Lexical Resolution Problem consists of one complete turn by the maximizer, and several failed attempts by the minimizer to reduce the complexity of the morpho-syntactic model.

In the first turn of this game, the maximizer [82, 85] outlines a sim-

---

[8] In some ways this language complexity game continues an old game that began in 1981 when the maximizer [32] formalized a restrictive model of language (generalized phrase structure grammar, or GPSG) based in ideas in [38] to capture certain long distance dependencies and proved that it was undecidable [80, 101]. The minimizer [81, 95] constrained the original GPSG model in a way that reduced its complexity to inside $\mathcal{NP}$ [81] and demonstrated that the restricted model was still capable of expressing the same facts of long distance dependencies. In 1985, the maximizer [33] significantly expanded the range of linguistic phenomena under consideration, resulting in a language model that was EXPPOLY-time hard [84]. The minimizer [84] replied with a revised model that was NP-complete, yet still capable of expressing the linguistic phenomena in question. The essential features of this "Revised GPSG" model were later captured in a simplified "agreement grammar" model [89], whose complexity was also shown to be NP-complete. Although this was a complexity game for formal languages (whose outcome strongly supports our complexity thesis), it cannot legitimately be considered a complexity game for human language, for the following reason. Each of the proposed GPSG models is weakly equivalent to the context-free languages (that is, the formal languages generated by the class of GPSG models were exactly the context-free languages). In fact, their "weak context-free generative power" was argued to be the primary merit of these GPSG models. However, context-free languages are grossly inadequate models of human language, being both too weak (incapable of representing basic facts of linguistic knowledge) and too strong (including infinitely many unnatural languages, and possessing arbitrarily many unnatural properties, such as closure under union). Although they have other merits, the GPSG models are therefore so grossly inadequate as models of human language that any complexity game involving them cannot reasonably be considered a true language complexity game.

ple model of the relation between the morphology and syntax, based on current transformational linguistic theory. The maximizer proves that the Lexical Resolution Problem is NP-hard in this model, and that it will be NP-hard in any such morpho-syntactic model with certain properties. To round out his turn, the maximizer shows how in detail how two morpho-syntactic models proposed in the linguistics literature (the Barriers model of Chomsky [19, 22] and the γ-marking model of Lasnik and Saito [62]) both have the properties in question, and therefore the Lexical Resolution Problem is NP-hard in those models. In the second turn, minimizer [85] considers a range of possible moves, ultimately rejecting them.

As of this writing then, three independent language complexity games have been played to a quiescent state. In each of the three games, the quiescent state is NP-completeness, which strongly supports our complexity thesis for human language.

Let us now begin our language complexity game, the language complexity game for anaphora.

2 The Anaphora Problem

This chapter begins a language complexity game defined by a fundamental problem in human language, that of determining the reference of the elements in linguistic representation. The question of how linguistic elements find their reference has been a central topic in the study of language and thought from the time of antiquity. However, this computational problem has not been precisely defined before, nor has its computational complexity been analyzed previously.

Some linguistic elements have what might be called "direct reference," because their reference is not mediated by other linguistic elements. These elements are called *referring-expressions*. Examples include proper nouns (for example, *Ann, John*) and definite noun phrases (for example, *my colleague, the man dressed in black*). The computational problem posed by these elements is to find a unique cognitive referent for each such element in a given linguistic representation. This is the Referential Interpretation Problem. For example, to represent the utterance *Romeo loved Juliet*, the language user might relate the proper nouns *Romeo* and *Juliet* to his mental representations of Romeo and Juliet, the star-crossed lovers of Shakespeare's famous tragedy.

Other linguistic elements, called *anaphoric elements*, have "indirect reference," because their reference depends on the reference of other linguistic elements. Examples of anaphoric elements include pronouns (for example, *he, they*), reflexives (for example, *himself, themselves*), and reciprocals (for example, *each other*). Anaphoric elements must have antecedents. The computational problem posed by these elements, then, is to find a unique (salient) antecedent for each anaphoric element in a given linguistic representation. This is the Anaphora Problem. For example, to represent the utterance *Narcissus adores himself*, the language user must determine that the proper noun *Narcissus* is the intended antecedent of the reflexive *himself*, and that therefore *himself* refers to whatever person *Narcissus* refers to.

The Anaphora Problem describes a pure language computation, whose output — an antecedence relation on linguistic elements — is entirely independent of other cognitive systems.[1] The Referential Interpretation

---

[1] Thus the language user may correctly assign an antecedent to every anaphoric element in a representation without determining the reference of any element in that representation. This is illustrated by the utterance *He adored himself so much that he fell in the pool when he saw his own reflection*. The language user may easily determine that the anaphoric elements in this utterance have the same reference without determining what that reference is. Therefore, the Anaphora Problem is

Problem, on the other hand, describes a computation whose output connects the language system to other cognitive systems.[2]

We depict a coreferential interpretation, where two linguistic elements α and β are understood as having the same reference, by assigning α the same subscript as β, as in *Narcissus$_1$ adores himself$_1$*. In each example, careful attention must be paid to the intended reference of the anaphoric elements, as indicated by the subscripts. For example, the utterance *Oedipus loved his mother* has two interpretations: one where *his* and *Oedipus* are coreferential, which we depict as *Oedipus$_1$ loved his$_1$ mother*; and a second interpretation where *his* refers to someone other that *Oedipus*, which we depict as *Oedipus$_1$ loved his$_2$ mother*.[3]

In some cases, two linguistic elements α and β may be judged to be obligatorily *disjoint* in reference. We depict such speaker-hearer judgements by assigning α the subscript of β preceeded by an asterisk, as in *Todd$_1$ hurt him$_{*1}$*.

Recall that language computations are defined by their outputs. In the case of the Anaphora Problem, the output consists of a unique (salient) relation of immediate antecedence. *Immediate antecedence* is an intransitive, asymmetric, irreflexive relation holding between an anaphoric element α and the linguistic element β from which it obtains its immediate linguistic reference, written $\mathsf{link}(\alpha, \beta)$. *Antecedence* is the positive transitive closure of the immediate antecedence relation, written $\mathsf{link}^+(\alpha, \beta)$.

---

independent of the Referential Interpretation Problem. Moreover, it is not possible to assign a reference to every element in a linguistic representation without first finding an antecedent for every anaphoric element in that representation. Therefore, the Anaphora Problem is a crucial subproblem of the Referential Interpretation Problem.

[2]The Referential Interpretation Problem, as broadly construed, is to determine the mental referent of every element in a linguistic representaion. Thus, we are led to postulate a universe $\mathcal{U}$ of mentally-represented referents that includes all nameable objects, entities, and concepts. Each referent in this cognitive universe is associated with certain properties, such as its conceptual, linguistic, and sensory-motor correlates. When the language user constructs a linguistic representation as part of the production, comprehension, or acquisition of a human language, he relates the elements in that linguistic representation to their intended referents in his cognitive universe of referents.

[3]Subscripts are simply a notation for representing speaker-hearer judgements. They should not to be confused with coindexing, an equivalence relation used by some linguists to represent coreference. Below we will argue that coreference — a transitive, symmetric, reflexive relation — is not directly represented in the language user. Rather, the language user represents the asymmetric antecedence relation from an anaphoric element to its linguistic antecedent. Two linguistic elements are judged to be coreferential when one is the linguistic antecedent of the other, or when they "accidentally corefer," as in *Bob$_1$ liked sushi, and Bob$_1$ also liked pickled ginger*. Accidental coreference is due to reference, a mentally-represented relation from a linguistic element to its cognitive referent. The relation of reference is entirely distinct from the relation of antecedence, which is relation defined on linguistic elements only.

Consider the utterance in (2).

(2) Tom_1 thought Mary said he_1 admired $himself_1$.

For reasons that will become clear in section 4.1.1 below, Tom_1 is the immediate antecedent of he_1 and he_1 is the immediate antecedent of $himself_1$ in the linguistic representation corresponding to the utterance (2). Therefore, by the transitivity of antecedence, Tom_1 is the antecedent of $himself_1$ in the linguistic representation for (2).

The output of this anaphora computation is a relation of immediate antecedence. What then is the input to the computation? And what correspondence between inputs and outputs is established by this language computation? The next section addresses these questions.

2.1 Defining the Problem

As stated above, the language user must determine the intended antecedent of every anaphoric element in a given utterance in order to successfully comprehend that utterance. However, the comprehender is not supplied with the producer's linguistic intentions, and if he were, then no language computation would be needed. Any success criterion based on the producer's intent can only be applied by an external observer with mystical access to the producer's and comprehender's mental representations. Therefore, any statement of the comprehension problem for anaphoric elements that involves the producer's intention cannot possibly be empirically plausible or technically coherent.

How then shall we define the anaphora problem?

According to our interpretation of language, language is a unitary computation from extralinguistic information to linguistic representations. Communication between two language users is successful only when their inputs (that is, the extralinguistic information available to them) are sufficiently similar to result in equivalent outputs (that is, linguistic representations). The unitary language computation may be described in terms of its component parts, each of which is a subcomputation from some linguistic and extralinguistic information to a representation of some component of linguistic knowledge. For example, the Anaphora Problem specifies a computation whose output is a relation of immediate antecedence. Therefore, the input to the Anaphora

Problem must be whatever linguistic and extralinguistic information is necessary to correctly determine a unique (salient) relation of immediate antecedence.

Let us consider the relevant linguistic information first. For one, the antecedent of each anaphoric element must be drawn from the set of antecedents available in the current utterance and in utterances produced earlier in the discourse. (Otherwise, every anaphoric element may be trivially assigned a distinct antecedent, none of which were previously mentioned in the discourse, which is the trivial *mis*comprehension problem for anaphoric elements.) Therefore, the input to the Anaphora Problem must include a set of available (salient) antecedents.

All other linguistic information relevant to the Anaphora Problem must be explicitly represented in a comprehensive linguistic representation. For these reasons, we define the broad *Anaphora Problem* to be: Given a linguistic representation R lacking only relations of referential dependency, and a set A^C of available antecedents, Output an antecedent in A^C for every anaphoric element in R. The set A^C of available antecedents models the discourse context in which the utterance is produced. The corresponding decision problem is to determine whether all the anaphoric elements in R can find their antecedents in A^C.

In the remainder of this chapter (and the subsequent two chapters as well), we explicitly model the linguistic information relevant to the computation of immediate antecedence, by means of language models that each characterize a set of possible linguistic representations. In particular, we construct five precise models of the broad Anaphora Problem, two based on the fact that anaphoric elements must agree in certain respects with their antecedents, and three based on the fact that pronouns must be disjoint in reference from certain potential antecedents.

However, linguistic information alone does not guarantee a unique salient output to the Anaphora Problem. More than one set of linkings may be consistent with the set A^C of available antecedents and the linguistic representation R, although only one will be salient to the language user. For example, when divorced from the context in which it was produced, the utterance *Bob thought Tom said he hated him* is ambiguous between the interpretation *Bob_1 thought Tom_2 said he_1 hated him_2* and the interpretation *Bob_1 thought Tom_2 said he_2 hated him_1*. The speaker intended exactly one of the two interpretations, and the hearer has no choice but to choose between the two interpretations on the basis of the extralinguistic information available to him, such as his knowledge about Bob, Tom, and the nature of their relationship.

Therefore, we must also model the extralinguistic information relevant to the computation of immediate antecedence. Although this input to the Anaphora Problem is poorly understood, we may be sure of one thing: extralinguistic information is relevant to the Anaphora Problem if and only if it demonstrably influences the output of the Anaphora Problem. That is, a subclass of the extralinguistic information is a relevant input to the Anaphora Problem if and only if it affects the selection of the antecedents of anaphoric elements. Therefore, we may accurately model the extralinguistic information by means of a preference function Υ that favors certain linkings over others, and thereby models the information available to the language user that we are otherwise unable to characterize in an empirically plausible manner.

For example, we may model certain semantic information with the preference function Υ. Anaphoric elements typically prefer to link to certain arguments over others, seemingly on the basis of the semantic roles assigned to those arguments. A semantic role specifies the role played by an object or entity in an activity or event. Some anaphoric elements may prefer to link to the initiator of an action (the so-called "agent" or "actor") rather than to the involuntary or passive participants in the action. This semantic preference function been studied extensively in recent work [35, 46], where it is called the thematic hierarchy.[4]

We would like to pick the weakest possible class of preference functions, in order to avoid introducing any unjustified complexity into our statement of the Anaphora Problem. Therefore, we will confine ourselves to the binary-valued preference function Υ, where $\Upsilon(\alpha, \beta)$ is 1 if and only if β is a preferred antecedent for the anaphoric element α, and 0 otherwise. We say that the preference value $\Upsilon(L)$ of a linking L is the number of anaphoric elements that are linked to one of their preferred

---

[4] A thematic hierarchy is a partial order on the set of possible semantic roles. Grimshaw [35] argues for the partial order

{agent} $\prec$ {experiencer} $\prec$ {goal, source, location} $\prec$ {theme},

while Jackendoff [46] argues for

{agent} $\prec$ {patient, beneficiary} $\prec$ {theme} $\prec$ {goal, source, location}.

The primary difference between these two proposals is whether the theme or the goal is the more preferred antecedent.

antecedents in L:[5]

$$\Upsilon(L) \doteq \sum_{(\alpha,\beta) \in L} \Upsilon(\alpha,\beta)$$

This leads to the following definition of the broad *Anaphoric Preference Problem*: Given a linguistic representation R lacking only relations of referential dependency, a set A^C of available antecedents, and a preference function Υ, output the maximally preferred linking L such that every anaphoric element in R has an antecedent in A^C. The corresponding decision problem is to determine whether or not there exists linking L such that every anaphoric element in R has an antecedent in A^C and $\Upsilon(L) \geq p_{\min}$ for a given representation R, available antecedents A^C, preference function Υ, and minimum preference value $p_{\min}$.

It should be clear that every instance of the Anaphora Problem along with the null preference function (that equally "prefers" every antecedent for every anaphoric element) is also an instance of the Anaphoric Preference Problem. In other words, the Anaphora Problem trivially reduces to the Anaphoric Preference Problem. Therefore, lower bounds on the Anaphora Problem are lower bounds on the Anaphoric Preference Problem, and upper bounds on the Anaphoric Preference Problem are upper bounds on the Anaphora Problem. In the remainder of this chapter we will confine our attention to the simple Anaphora Problem, confident that our complexity lower bounds also apply to the more accurate Anaphoric Preference Problem. In chapter 5, we will discuss the complexity of the Anaphoric Preference Problem with respect to two models of syntactic ellipsis.

It should be equally clear that we have not significantly increased the complexity of the Anaphora Problem by including the binary-valued preference function Υ (or even its more general nonnegative integer-valued counterpart). In either case, the problem of finding the maximally preferred linking given such a preference function and no additional linguistic information may be solved by choosing the most preferred link for each anaphoric element in complete isolation, which may be done

---

[5] We may also wish to consider a slightly more general class of preference functions, each of which assigns a nonnegative integral value to every possible relation of immediate antecedence, indicating the degree $\Upsilon(\alpha,\beta)$ to which a linguistic element β is the preferred antecedent of an anaphoric element α. The preference of a complete linking L would also be the sum of the preferences assigned to each link relation in L.

in time proportional to the size of (the chosen representation of) the preference function.

This concludes our discussion of how to define the Anaphora Problem. Before turning to chapter 3, and our first language model for the Anaphora Problem, two caveats are in order.

2.2 Discussion

In this monograph we only consider language problems, which are abstract descriptions of computations that must be performed in the comprehension, production, or acquistion of human languages. Language problems, such as the Anaphora Problem, must not be confused with the problem of determining the 'truth' (or 'truth conditions') of linguistic utterances. The language user need not know or believe that '$John_1$ saw $John_1$' to comprehend the utterance *John saw himself* as $John_1$ *saw himself*$_1$.

Nor should our language problems be confused with mental puzzles informally described using the utterances of a natural language. In particular, the Anaphora Problem should not be confused with so-called "word problems." The Anaphora Problem is an abstract description of a class of computations that must be performed in order to comprehend the utterances of a human language. In contrast, a word problem is an abstract problem or puzzle that is described informally in a natural language, such as those found on standardized exams or in books by E.R. Emmet [28].[6] The language user need not solve these word problems in order to comprehend their natural language description. More generally, the language user need not solve such word problems in order to comprehend or produce the utterances of his language. However, the

---

[6] For example, consider the following discourse, based on [28, p.7]: "Andy, Bob, David, Eric, and Gary have their birthdays on consecutive days, but not necessarily in that order. Andy's birthday is as many days before Gary's as Bob's is after Eric's. David is two days older than Eric. Gary's birthday this year is on a Wednesday. This year, Eric celebrated his birthday at a Japanese restaurant." In order to comprehend the last sentence in the discourse, the language user must (unconsciously) answer the question, "What is the the antecedent of the pronoun *his* in the utterance *Eric celebrated his birthday at a Japanese restaurant?*," even though the answer to that question is not uniquely determined by the discourse. This is an instance of the Anaphora Problem. In contrast, the language user need not answer the question "What day of the week did Eric's birthday fall on this year?," even though the answer to that question ("Tuesday") is completely determined by the discourse. This is a word problem. Other examples may be found in [27, 30] and in public libraries under subject headings such as "Puzzles" and "Mathematical Recreations."

language user *must* solve the Anaphora Problem in order to comprehend or produce the utterances of his language.

Finally, it is not to be expected that the utterances constructed below are easy to comprehend or produce, any more than we expect to actually build the physical devices used to prove lower bounds on the complexity of problems in robot motion planning [12, 77, 78]. Certainly, it is not possible to build physical devices of such intricacy, any more than it is easy for a language user to comprehend or produce the utterances we construct below. Yet the practical questions of what physical devices can and cannot be built, or of what linguistic expressions can and cannot be easily understood in everyday discourse do not concern us here. We want to understand the theoretical structure of language computations and we use complexity analysis to better reveal this structure.

2.3 Summary of Anaphora Results

Our technical results related to the Anaphora Problem may be summarized as follows.

In chapter 3 we model the agreement constraint holding between an anaphoric element and its antecedent. First the maximizer proves that the Anaphora Problem is NP-hard under a widely accepted model of anaphoric agreement called the "standard agreement condition" (SAC). The SAC accounts for basic facts of anaphoric antecedence, for example, that the masculine singular pronoun *his* cannot refer to the feminine singular antecedent *the woman* in the utterance *The woman$_1$ ate his$_{*1}$ breakfast*, although the feminine singular pronoun *her* can in the otherwise identical utterance *The woman$_1$ ate her$_1$ breakfast*. With the insight gained from our complexity analysis, the minimizer presents counterexamples to the SAC and offers an improved model of anaphoric agreement under which the Anaphora Problem is provably contained in $\mathcal{P}$.

Next, in chapter 4 we model the referential dependencies in a comprehensive linguistic representation. The maximizer proves the NP-hardness of the Anaphora Problem under a more robust model, the referential dependency model. This model is based directly on the fact that certain arguments in an utterance must be understood as being coreferential or disjoint in reference. These facts about language user's conscious knowledge of referential dependency are established using well-understood, uncontroversial empirical arguments from linguistics. For this reason, we may believe with confidence that this NP-hardness result applies to all adequate linguistic theories, and that it establishes the NP-hardness of the unitary language computation as a whole.

Finally, in chapter 5 we model the interaction between anaphora and syntactic ellipsis. The maximizer shows how a widely-accepted theory of syntactic ellipsis leads to a proof that the Anaphora Problem is PSPACE-hard. Next, the minimizer falsifies this linguistic theory with counterexamples, and sketches a descriptively superior account of ellipsis that reduces the complexity of the Anaphora Problem to $\mathcal{NP}$. This constitutes evidence for an $\mathcal{NP}$ upper bound on the Anaphora Problem, because ellipsis is arguably the most computationally complex phenomenon in the syntax of human languages.

3 Anaphoric Agreement

Language users know that an anaphoric element α may inherit the reference of an argument β, as in *Todd hurt himself*, where the reflexive *himself* is understood as referring to the proper noun *Todd*, or *Todd said Mary liked him*, which could mean that 'Todd said Mary liked Todd'. Recall that the judgement of coreference between α and its antecedent β is depicted here by assigning α and β the same subscript. Careful attention must be paid to the intended interpretation of the anaphoric elements in the examples below, as indicated by the subscripts.

Language users also know that an anaphoric element must agree with its antecedent with respect to certain inflectional distinctions, such as person, number and gender. This fact is briefly illustrated in (3) for third person singular reflexives, and in (4) for third person singular pronouns.

(3) a. The man$_1$ liked himself$_1$.
   b. * The woman$_1$ liked himself$_1$.

(4) a. * The man$_1$ thought Bill liked her$_1$.
   b. The woman$_1$ thought Bill liked her$_1$.

The asterisk '*' is used in (3b,4a) to indicate the impossibility of the depicted interpretation.

The agreement constraint does not require exact identity of agreement features. The anaphoric element may be more specific than its antecedent, as illustrated in (5), where the anaphoric elements (*his, her*) are inflected for gender, but their antecedent (*the student*) is not.

(5) The student$_1$ studied hard for his$_1$/her$_1$ exam.

The anaphoric element also may be more general than its antecedent, as illustrated in (6), where the anaphoric element is not inflected for gender, although its antecedents are.

(6) The men$_1$/women$_1$ were proud of their$_1$ work.

This suggests that the agreement constraint is based on unification of inflectional features: an anaphoric element agrees with its antecedent only if they do not disagree on the value of any inflectional feature [104]. (We will use "agreement feature" and "inflectional feature" interchangeably, for reasons that will become clear below in section 3.3.)

The agreement constraint is transitive, as illustrated by the examples in (7), where *the student* can be masculine (7a) or feminine (7b), but not both simultaneously (7c).

(7) a. The student$_1$ prepared her$_1$ breakfast
 b. The student$_1$ did his$_1$ homework.
 c. *The student$_1$ prepared her$_1$ breakfast after doing his$_1$ homework.

The goal of this chapter is to precisely model this constraint on anaphoric agreement. In section 3.1, the maximizer proposes an agreement model based on a simple theory widely accepted in generative, computational and structuralist linguistics. In section 3.2, the maximizer proves that the Anaphora Problem is NP-complete according to this standard agreement model. In section 3.3, the minimizer falsifies this standard agreement model and proposes an alternate model based on the newly-developed theory of paradigm structure. Finally, in section 3.4, the Anaphora Problem is proven to be quadratic time according to this anaphoric uniqueness model.

3.1 The Standard Agreement Model

Knowledge of coreference and the agreement constraint must be represented in the language user, and hence by every scientifically plausible language model as well. The simplest and least controversial representation is to postulate an abstract linguistic relation between an anaphoric element and its linguistic antecedent, governed by an agreement constraint defined over a set of relevant agreement features. Let us make these ideas precise.

Following Higginbotham [39], we may formalize the notion of immediate antecedence with an assymetric link(α, β) relation between an anaphoric element α and its immediate antecedent β, subject to the agreement condition. Let link$^+$ be the positive transitive closure of the directed link relation. link is the relation of immediate antecedence; link$^+$ is the relation of antecedence.

We have seen that an anaphoric element and its antecedent must agree in certain respects. This requirement may be formalized as follows. Let a *feature* be a [feature-name feature-value] pair, such as [gender masculine]. Features are a formalization of the notion "relevant linguistic distinction." Every linguistic element is associated with a set of such features, called a *category*. Two elements are *nondistinct* if and only if their feature sets do not disagree on any common featurename (that is, their inflectional categories may be unified).

The facts of interpretation illustrated in (3–7) above may be described as the *Standard Agreement Condition* (SAC): all anaphoric elements that share an antecedent must be nondistinct from it and from each other.[1] This theory of anaphoric agreement is widely accepted in many branches of linguistics, and has not to the author's knowledge been controverted.

Anaphoric elements in different languages are marked for a wide range of distinctions in person, gender, number, animacy, case, social class, kinship, reference, antecedent noun class, grammatical function, thematic role, and so on [93, 106]. It is true that every particular language contains a fixed number of such inflectional (or agreement) features. However, linguistic theory properly idealizes to an unbounded number of agreement features because these features and the range of their possible values varies considerably from language to language and does not seem to be restricted in principle [75, 76, 85].

In section 2.1, we defined the Anaphora Problem as the problem of finding an antecedent for every anaphoric element in a linguistic representation R. We have seen that the configurations among the arguments in a linguistic representation can affect the link relations that are possible for that representation. For example, *him* can refer to *John* in the utterance *John$_1$ said Mary saw him$_1$* but not in the utterance *John$_1$ saw him$_{*1}$*. In section 4.1 below, we study how certain configurations in a linguistic representation are mapped into relations referential dependencies, in total isolation from the intrinsic properties of the linguistic elements involved. However, in this section we study how the intrinsic agreement properties of linguistic elements affect the Anaphora Problem, in total isolation from the extrinsic properties of those elements in a given linguistic representation. In order to do that, we must essentially ignore the structural relations between elements in the linguistic representation.

For these reasons, we define the Anaphora Problem in this agreement model ("Anaphoric Agreement") as follows. The input consists of a 3-tuple $\langle A^A, A^B, A^C \rangle$ of disjoint sets of arguments, where A^A consists of

---

[1] Our Standard Agreement Condtion (SAC) should not be confused with the Syntactic Agreement Constraint (SAC) of Bosch [11], to which it is in no way related.

reflexives and reciprocals, A^B consists of pronouns, and A^C consists of referring-expressions.[2] A^C is the set of available antecedents, and $A \doteq A^A \cup A^B \cup A^C$ is the universe of linguistic arguments in the hypothetical linguistic representation. The output is an available antecedent for each anaphoric element in A that does not violate the SAC. More precisely, the output is a set of links $L \subset (A^A \cup A^B) \times A$ such that (i) every anaphoric element $\alpha \in (A^A \cup A^B)$ has an ultimate antecedent $\beta \in A^C$ such that $\text{link}^+(\alpha, \beta) \in L^+$ and (ii) $\text{link}^+(\alpha_1, \beta) \in L^+$ and $\text{link}^+(\alpha_2, \beta) \in L^+$ only if α_1, α_2, and β are nondistinct.

This problem statement does not exclude circular dependencies [39], as in (8a), nor does it allow split antecedents, as in (8b).

(8) a. *[his$_2$ mother]$_1$ liked [her$_1$ father]$_2$.
   b. John$_1$ told Bill$_2$ that they$_{\{1,2\}}$ should do the right thing.

Although it is straightforward to exclude circular dependencies, such linking structures are not related to the intrinsic agreement properties of anaphoric elements, and so we do not consider them here. The exact conditions governing anaphoric agreement with split antecedents are poorly understood; see fn.1 in section 4.1 below for a cursory discussion of the difficulties involved. Many languages do not permit split antecedents, and so our definition of the Anaphoric Agreement Problem is none the less relevant to human language as a whole.

To recapitulate, this statement of the Anaphoric Agreement Problem ignores the structural relations between anaphoric elements, because the SAC refers only to the intrinsic properties of an anaphoric element and its antecedents. The SAC is not sensitive to the structural relations between anaphoric elements and their antecedents: it merely requires that their agreement features not disagree. For this specialization of the Anaphora Problem, it therefore makes sense to essentially ignore the relations holding between linguistic elements.[3]

---

[2] We have partitioned the class of possible thematic arguments into subclasses according to their referential properties with respect to the binding conditions A, B, and C (see section 4.1 below). And so the notation A^A is intended to suggest the set of arguments subject to binding condition A (that is, reflexives and reciprocals); A^B to suggest the set of arguments subject to binding condition B (that is, pronouns); and A^C the set of arguments subject to binding condition C (that is, referring-expressions).

[3] Although we have reduced the input to the Anaphora Problem to sets of linguistic elements, in complete isolation from the linguistic representation in which they appear, every instance of this Anaphoric Agreement Problem may be trivially

3.2 From Graph Coloring to Anaphoric Agreement

The fact that all anaphoric elements that share an antecedent must agree with it and with each other, in combination with the fact that anaphoric elements must have antecedents, suffices to establish the following lemma.

LEMMA 1 Graph k-coloring $\leq_\mathcal{P}$ Anaphoric Agreement.

Proof 1 On input k colors and a graph $G = \langle V, E \rangle$ with vertices $V = \{v_1, v_2, \ldots, v_n\}$ and edges E, our reduction ρ outputs a 3-tuple $\rho(G) = \langle A^A, A^B, A^C \rangle$ of disjoint sets of arguments, where A^A is empty, A^B consists of $|V|$ pronouns, and A^C consists of k referring-expressions such that G is k-colorable if and only if the pronouns A^B can be linked to the k available antecedents A^C without violating the standard agreement condition.

The idea of the reduction is to map colors into available antecedents in A^C, vertices in the graph G into pronouns in A^B, and edges in the graph G into disagreement between the pronouns in A^B. To do this we need the n binary agreement feature-names $\varphi_1, \varphi_2, \ldots, \varphi_n$; the pronouns $p_1, p_2, \ldots, p_n$; and the available antecedents $R_1, R_2, \ldots, R_k$. Each R_i is a referring-expression, such as a noun phrase, that is not specified for any of the n chosen agreement feature-names. Pronoun p_i represents vertex v_i: for each edge $(v_i, v_j) \in E$ incident with vertex v_i, pronoun p_i has $\varphi_i = 0$ and pronoun p_j has $\varphi_i = 1$.

By the definition of the Anaphora Problem, every pronoun in A^B must refer to one of the k available antecedents in A^C. If there is an edge between two vertices in the input graph G, then those two corresponding pronouns cannot share an antecedent in A^C without disagreeing on some agreement feature (by construction). Therefore each correct linking from

---

mapped into an equivalent instance of the broad Anaphora Problem. That is, any 3-tuple $A = \langle A^A, A^B, A^C \rangle$ of disjoint sets of arguments may be easily mapped into a natural linguistic representation R where every referring-expression in R is a possible antecedent for each anaphoric element in R, and R does not give rise to any relations of referential dependency that interfere with free reign of the agreement conditions. This may be accomplished in three steps. First, make each pronoun in A^B and each referring-expression in A^C arguments of their own verbs, which will make them nonlocal. Second, make each $\alpha \in A^A$ the direct object of its own verb with the subject of that verb a "dummy" pronoun β that agrees exactly with α. This configuration forces α to link β, and then β is free to find any antecedent for α, subject only to the agreement condition. Third, make sure that none of the A^A or A^B c-commands any of the A^C, which is always trivial to accomplish, as we did in example (7).

the pronouns to the available antecedents exactly corresponds to a k-coloring of the input graph G. □

The reduction uses n binary agreement feature-names, one for each vertex in the graph. The feature system is used to represent subsets of the n vertices, and therefore must be capable of making an exponential number of distinctions. (In terms of the input length $m = |G|$, this feature system is capable of making $2^{\sqrt{m}}$ distinctions.)

ccording to the SAC, anaphoric agreement is NP-complete: NP-hard by lemma 1, because the graph coloring problem is NP-complete [48], and in $\mathcal{NP}$ straightforwardly (guess a unique antecedent for each anaphoric element, propagate agreement features along links, and then check for agreement conflicts).

Before asserting that Anaphora Problem (and therefore the unitary language computation as a whole) is really NP-hard, it behooves us to more critically examine the linguistic analysis upon which our complexity analysis is based.

3.3 Agreement Reconsidered

In linguistics, agreement is nearly always stated in terms of feature unification: two linguistic elements agree if and only if they do not disagree on any feature value. This Standard Agreement Condition makes a broad empirical claim, namely, that anaphoric elements can share an antecedent when they do not disagree on any agreement features. Let us evaluate this claim.

The requirement that coreferential elements be nondistinct may be broken into three subcases. Two linguistic elements are nondistinct if and only if (a) they are *orthogonal* (that is, they have no common feature-name); (b) one *subsumes* the other (that is, one is strictly more general than the other); or (c) they *partially overlap* (that is, they have some but not all features in common):

(9) a. { [number plural] }, { [gender masculine] }
   b. { [number plural] }, { [number plural], [gender masculine] }
   c. { [number singular], [person 1] },
      { [number singular], [gender masculine] }

The strongest confirmation of the SAC, then, would be to find languages for each of the three subcases of nondistinctness: languages with orthogonal anaphoric elmements, languages with anaphoric elements that subsume each other, and languages with anaphoric elements that partially overlap. If such languages do not exist, then the SAC cannot be falsified, and it should be abandoned in favor of a simpler theory because it is unnecessarily powerful. One such simpler theory of anaphoric agreement would be that two anaphoric elements can share an antecedent if and only if their agreement features are identical.

According to accepted linguistic thought, English is not such a language, nor could we find such a language among those spoken in Europe, or in the forty nine non-European languages discussed in a prominent cross-linguistic study of pronominal systems [106]. These languages are all alleged to have pronominal paradigms that can be written down in the standard textbook format, as a chart that partitions the space of possible feature combinations.

For example, the paradigm for English personal pronouns appears to exactly partition the space of possible combinations of inflectional features, as shown in figure 3.1 (suppressing case marking).[4]

		singular	plural
1st		*I*	*we*
2nd		*you*	
3rd	masc	*he*	*they*
	fem	*she*	
	neut	*it*	

Figure 3.1
According to conventional thought, the system (or paradigm) of English personal pronouns exactly partitions the space of possible inflectional categories.

However, a more thorough investigation of the system of English personal pronouns suggests that *he* subsumes *she* in many idiolects, and that in some idiolects *they* subsumes *he/she* as well.

There is some evidence that *he* subsumes *she*. For most English speakers, the utterance *Mark$_1$ hates his$_1$ neighbors and so does Mary$_2$* is am-

---

[4]The pronoun *one* is not a supporting example for the SAC (and hence not a counterexample to our claim), because it does not have a linguistic antecedent. Rather, it has an "arbitrary" interpretation and may only accidentally corefer.

biguous between the "invariant" reading paraphrased in (10a) and the "covariant" reading paraphrased in (10b).

(10) a. Mark$_1$ hates his$_1$ neighbors and so does Mary$_2$ *hate his$_1$ neighbors*.
b. Mark$_1$ hates his$_1$ neighbors and so does Mary$_2$ *hate her$_2$ neighbors*.

However, for many native speakers the virtually identical utterance *Mary$_1$ hates her$_1$ neighbors and so does Max$_2$* only has the invariant reading paraphrased in (11a). The covariant reading in (11b), where both Mary and Max are understood as hating their own neighbors, is not available to those speakers.[5]

(11) a. Mary$_1$ hates her$_1$ neighbors and so does Max$_2$ *hate her$_1$ neighbors*.
b. * Mary$_1$ hates her$_1$ neighbors and so does Max$_2$ *hate his$_2$ neighbors*.

For speakers whose judgments agree with the interpretations shown, the pronoun *his* is the pure third person singular pronoun, unspecified for gender, that therefore subsumes *she*, which is additionally specified for feminine gender. However, no English speaker may use *he* and *she* to refer to the same antecedent in the same utterance — recall example (7) above — contra the Standard Agreement Condition.

There is also evidence that *they* subsumes *he/she*, at least for some English speakers in some situations. Imagine the following scenario. You are talking to a new friend about his recent health checkup, and, not wishing to make any sexist assumptions about the gender of the examining doctor, you use the third person pronoun *they* (12a) instead of either third person singular pronoun (12b).

(12) a. About your doctor$_1$, do they$_1$ seem competent?
b. About your doctor$_1$, does he$_1$/she$_1$ examine you thoroughly?

In example (12a), *they* is used as a pure third person pronoun, unmarked for number or gender, that therefore subsumes both *he* and *she*.[6] (Ex-

---

[5]The asymmetry between *his* and *her* with respect to the possibility of a covariant intepretation has recently has been investigated in considerable depth [53].

[6]The marginal possibility of a covariant interpretation for *Your doctor$_1$ [seemed competent when they$_1$ examined you] and your accountants$_2$ did [e] too* is potentially additional supporting evidence for the claim that *they* is the pure third person pronoun, unspecified for number or gender. However, the covariant interpretation is considerably more difficult to obtain when the present tense is used, and the ostensibly plural NP *your accountants* may be underlyingly singular, as in *your (team of) accountants*.

ample (12a) is all the more curious because the matrix subject *they* refers to the singular noun *doctor* while agreeing with the plural auxiliary *do*.)

The examples (13) demonstrate that it is not possible to use *they* in combination with *he* or *she*, contra the Standard Agreement Condition.

(13) a. About your doctor$_1$, do they$_1$ seem competent when he$_{*1}$/she$_{*1}$ examines you?
 b. About your doctor$_1$, does he$_1$/she$_1$ seem competent when they$_{*1}$ examine you?

The fact that neither pronoun order is possible in (13) — more general *they* before more specific *he/she* in (13a), or vice versa in (13b) — establishes that Wasow's Novelty Condition [103, 108] is not a factor here. The Novelty Condition states that an anaphoric element cannot be more specific that its antecedent(s).

In short, if *he* subsumes *she* in any English dialect, as we have argued it does, then the SAC is false because *he* and *she* are nondistinct yet can never share an antecedent. The same argument holds for *they* and the pronouns that it appears to subsume (that is, *he/she*).

Let us summarize our empirical critique of the SAC. It appears that no known human language has anaphoric elements that partially overlap or are completely disjoint, and hence two important empirical predictions of the SAC cannot be falsified or confirmed. Some English speakers have a paradigm of personal pronouns where one pronoun subsumes a second pronoun, yet both cannot refer to the same antecedent in the same utterance. For this reason, the one remaining empirical prediction of the SAC is falsified. In short, the SAC is an inadequate theory of anaphoric agreement.

The fact that *he* subsumes *she* and that *they* may subsume all third person personal pronouns is not all that surprising when we consider other paradigms of human language. In the next section, we reduce the anaphoric agreement condition to the independently-motivated theory of paradigm structure. We will show how the agreement constraints holding between anaphoric elements and their antecedents may be explained entirely as arising from the paradigm structure of anaphoric elements.

3.3.1 Theory of Paradigm Structure

Informally, a paradigm is an array containing the inflected forms of a given word, such as a conjugation of verbs or a declension of nouns. More abstractly, then, the paradigm for a given word is a mapping from a set of inflectional features to the linguistic form of that word that realizes those features. (In figure 3.1, we diagramed the three-dimensional paradigm for English personal pronouns, as it is conventionally understood.)

Recall that a category is a set of inflectional features. Then, following Williams [109], we may visualize a paradigm as a tree of inflectional categories, where all categories at a given level in the tree are specified for the same inflectional features, and each category in the tree dominates all categories that it subsumes. Therefore, each leaf node represents a complete set of inflectional features, each interior node represents a partial set of features, and the root node represents the empty set (that is, the most general category). Each node in this tree, whether interior or leaf, may (potentially) contain a linguistic form. Given an inflectional category c, the paradigm outputs the linguistic form α contained in the most specific node in the tree that subsumes c. Equivalently, α is the linguistic form contained in the node that most closely dominates the category c in this tree. (The relations of subsumption and domination are reflexive, asymmetric and transitive.) It is not uncommon for a path from the root node to a leaf node to include two nodes that each contain a distinct linguistic form, for example, in cases of blocking and suppletion. The hypothesized paradigm structures for English personal pronouns are depicted in figure 3.2.

Let us formalize the notion of a paradigm. To do so, we must first formalize the system of inflectional features, a portion of universal grammar. The universal *inflectional feature system* is a 4-tuple $\langle F_u, V_u, \prec_u, \rho \rangle$, where F_u is the set of possible inflectional feature-names, V_u is the set of possible inflectional feature-values, $\prec_u$ is a total order on the feature-names F_u, and $\rho : F_u \to V_u$ defines the set of valid features. Recall that a *feature* is a [feature-name feature-value] pair. A feature $[f\ v]$ is *valid* iff $f \in F_u$, $v \in V_u$, and $v \in \rho(f)$. A *category* is a set of valid features, or more accurately, a valid partial function from the set of feature-names to the set of feature-values. If a category c is not defined for a given feature-name f, then $c(f) = \texttt{nil}$; otherwise, the category c is defined for the feature-name f, and $c(f) \in \rho(f)$. A category c is *valid*

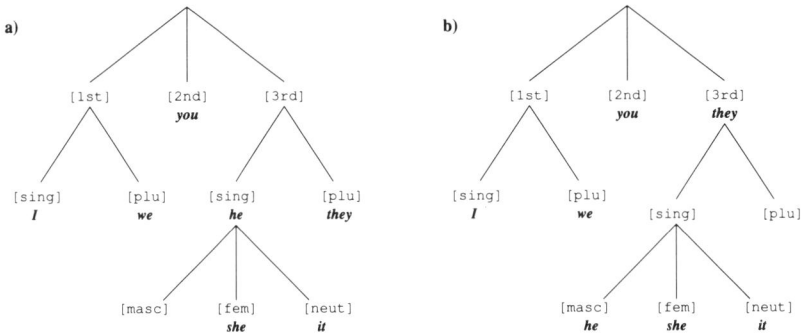

Figure 3.2
Two extant paradigms for English personal pronouns are depicted. Given an antecedent β with agreement features c, the paradigm requires the English speaker to choose the most specific pronoun whose inflectional features dominate c. In the more common paradigm on the left, *he* dominates *she* and hence *he* will take third person singular antecedents, as well as third person singular masculine antecedents. In the less common paradigm on the right, *they* dominates all nodes in the third person subtree, and hence will take third person singular antecedents with unknown gender, as well as third person plural antecedents.

iff it obeys the total order $\prec_u$, that is, if and only if

$$\forall f_i, f_j \in F_u[(f_i \prec_u f_j) \wedge (c(f_j) \in \rho(f_j)) \Rightarrow c(f_i) \in \rho(f_i)].$$

The inflectional feature system defines a universal set $\mathcal{C}$ of valid inflectional categories.

Recall that a paradigm is a language-particuar mapping from a set of valid inflectional categories to a set of related linguistic forms. To be precise, a paradigm structure P is a 4-tuple $P = \langle F, V, W, \lambda \rangle$, where $F \subseteq F_u$ and $V \subseteq V_u$ are the sets of inflectional feature-names and feature-values (respectively) employed in the language, W is a set of related linguistic forms (such as the inflected forms of a word), and $\lambda : C \to W$ is the language-particular paradigm labeling function, a partial function. The feature-names F and the feature-values V define the set $C \subseteq \mathcal{C}$ of valid inflectional categories. We represent the labeling function λ as a relation, that is, as a proper subset of $C \times W$.

The paradigm structure P extends the partial function λ to a total function on C, as follows. Given a valid category $c \in C$, $P(c)$ is the linguistic form that labels the most specific valid category that subsumes c. That is, $P(c)$ is the unique linguistic form $w \in W$ such that

$$\exists a \in C[a \subseteq c \land \lambda(a) = w \land \forall b \in C[a \subset b \land b \subseteq c \land \lambda(b) = \texttt{nil}]]$$

In the absence of empirical counterevidence, we have made the language-universal order $\prec_u$ a total order on the inflectional features rather than a partial order. This is the stronger, more easily falsified hypothesis. If universal grammar only imposes a partial order on the inflectional features, then our model of the paradigm structure must be augmented to allow each particular language to extend the language-universal partial order $\prec_u$ to a language-particular total order. The complexity results in this monograph are independent of this choice.

A model of paradigm structure must satisfy three scientific criteria. First, it must be capable of representing all and only the humanly possible word paradigms. Second, it must predict actual historical changes in word paradigms. Third, it must allow the language learner to correctly predict the unattested forms in a paradigm. By these criteria, the null model of paradigm structure is a set of pairs $\langle c, w \rangle$, where c is a fully-specified inflectional category and w is its linguistic form. Although such a model is descriptively adequate, its predictions for language change and language acquisition are extremely weak. Likely historical changes are limited to those that change the second element of pair in P, for example, changing $\langle c, w \rangle$ to $\langle c, x \rangle$, $x \neq w$. The model says that all paradigms are equally easy to learn, and that the language user does not predict the forms of unattested inflectional categories (that is, the language learner does not generalize from the attested forms of a paradigm.)

In addition to being descriptively adequate, our proposed model of paradigm structure makes stronger predictions for language change and language acquisition than the null model does. Likely historical changes are those that involve small changes in the labeling function λ, such as those that move a linguistic form up or down in the paradigm tree, or those that change the form associated to a given category in the paradigm tree. The model says that paradigms containing fewer category labels (and hence fewer distinct linguistic forms) are easier to learn. Thus, the language user may predict the forms of unattested inflectional categories by always assigning an attested form to the most general category consistent with the observed linguistic evidence.[7]

---

[7]Many alternate models of paradigm structure have recently been proposed in the generative morphology literature, for example, [2, 37, 65, 73]. Although these models are all considerably more sophisticated than our model, they are also more powerful, and it is not clear whether they in fact make stronger or more accurate predictions

The next step in our investigation is to relate the facts of anaphoric agreement to the formal theory of paradigm structure.

3.3.2 Paradigms for Anaphoric Elements

Anaphoric elements with different conceptual semantics or that entail different relations of referential dependency are contained in different anaphoric paradigms. In particular, languages invariably have separate paradigms for reciprocals and personal pronouns. In addition, a language has separate paradigms for each of the reflexives that it allows [55] (local reflexives, medium-distance reflexives, and/or long-distance reflexives). These paradigms are all defined on the same set F of inflectional feature-names and V of feature-values. For example, English dialects permit only one (local) linking domain for reflexives, and therefore contain exactly three paradigms for anaphoric elements: one each for reflexives, reciprocals, and personal pronouns. These paradigms all obey the same total order on the same inflectional features: **person** $\prec$ **number** $\prec$ **gender**. For the sake of simplicity, we will henceforth combine the English paradigms for reflexives and reciprocals into one paradigm.

The facts of anaphoric agreement may be summarized in the following *Anaphoric Uniqueness Condition* (AUC): A linguistic element β whose inflectional category in c may be the antecedent of an anaphoric element α contained in the paradigm P if and only if $P(c) = \alpha$.

The immediate consequence of the AUC is that a linguistic element β can only be the antecedent of the anaphoric form contained in the most specific node in the paradigm structure that dominates the inflectional features of the element β. The AUC guarantees that an antecedent can only be shared among anaphoric elements from different paradigms. Two anaphoric elements from the same paradigm structure may never share an antecedent, while two anaphoric elements from the same paradigm structure may share an antecedent if and only if each independently agrees with the antecedent. Anaphoric agreement is an entirely local condition between an anaphoric element and its ultimate antecedent.

The AUC will correctly account for all the agreement examples discussed above in section 3.1. In addition, the AUC describes the contrast between the examples (12) and (14).

---

for language change and language acquisition.

(14) a. About Bob$_1$, did they$_{*1}$ like sailing?
   b. About Bob$_1$, did he$_1$/she$_{*1}$ like sailing?

Even though the pronoun *they* subsumes the proper noun *Bob* in (14a), *they* still cannot refer to *Bob* because the pronoun *he* subsumes *Bob* as well, and *he* is more specific than *they* in all idiolects.

Three apparent difficulties remain. One apparent exception to the AUC are the examples in (12), where *the doctor* can be the antecedent of *he*, *she*, or *they*. These exceptions trade on the ambiguous inflectional features (and reference) of the animate noun *doctor* and hence are only apparent. (See fn.2, p.22 above for a brief discussion of reference.) Once the inflectional features of the noun *doctor* are fixed in the language user's representation, as they must be, the gender of the *doctor* is also fixed as either unspecified or specified masculine or feminine. Then the appropriate anaphoric element for *doctor* is uniquely determined by the paradigm structures for English anaphoric elements. In other words, when the agreement features of an antecedent are ambiguous to the language user, then he may freely choose what agreement features are assigned to that antecedent in his representation of the given utterance. However, the language user must (eventually) settle on a unique choice consistent with the antecedent relations in the representation of that utterance.

A second apparent difficulty is that the third person pronoun *they* must be the immediate antecedent of the third person plural reciprocal *each other* in the utterance *They admired each other*, despite the fact that *each other* is more specific that *they* (see figure 3.2 above). This is in apparent contradiction to the AUC, which requires anaphoric elements to link to antecedents that are more general. This fact requires us to explicitly model the discourse context within which an utterance is produced. We simply extend the set A^C of available antecedents to include a set of salient mental referents with known inflectional features. Returning to our example utterance *They$_1$ admired each other$_1$*, we would say that the set of available antecedents includes a "silent" third person plural argument, that was uttered earlier in the discourse and is still available as an antecedent.

The third apparent difficulty is that the ellipsed pronoun *his* is understood as referring to the overt antecedent *Mary* in the covariant interpetation (10b). It would therefore seem that *his* and *Mary* agree, contra the AUC. According to the AUC, the existence of the feminine singular pronoun *her*, which is more specific than the pure singular pronoun *his* and at least as general as the feminine singular antecedent *Mary*, implies that *his* does not agree with *Mary*. Clearly, this is the correct result for overt anaphoric elements, and therefore something special must be said about the agreement constraints involved in the covariant intepretation of ellipsed anaphoric elements. We return to this question in section 5.4 below.[8]

The Anaphora Problem under the AUC ("Anaphoric Uniqueness") is defined as follows. The input consists of paradigms P_A, P_B for anaphoric elements along with a 3-tuple (A^A, A^B, A^C) of disjoint sets of arguments, where A^A consists of reflexives and reciprocals, A^B consists of pronouns, and A^C consists of referring-expressions. As above, A^C is the set of available antecedents, each marked with its intrinsic agreement features, while $A \doteq A^A \cup A^B \cup A^C$ is the universe of thematic arguments in the hypothetical linguistic representation. The output is an antecedent for each anaphoric element. More precisely, the output is a set of link relations $L \subset (A^A \cup A^B) \times A^C$ such that every anaphoric element $\alpha \in (A^A \cup A^B)$ has a unique antecedent $\beta \in A^C$ such that $P_{A/B}(\beta) = \alpha$.[9]

Let us now determine the complexity of the Anaphora Problem according to the Anaphoric Uniqueness Condition, our revised theory of anaphoric agreement.

3.4 An Upper Bound on Anaphoric Uniqueness

Recall that lemma 1 was established with respect to the Standard Agreement Condition. If the Standard Agreement Condition is false empirically, as we have argued it is, then the maximizer's model of anaphoric

---

[8] Our idea, in simplest terms, follows. In a covariant interpretation, the inflectional features of the ellipsed anaphoric element become part of the selectional restrictions imposed on its overt antecedent. Let α be an ellipsed anaphoric element whose understood antecedent in a covariant interpretation is the overt argument β. Let β be assigned the thematic argument position i. We represent this interpretation as a relation of immediate antecedence from α to the thematic position i. Then the inflectional features of α are included in the selectional restrictions imposed on β by i. The net effect is that the inflectional features of an ellipsed anaphoric element must subsume those of its overt antecedent(s) in a covariant interpretation, which is a weaker constraint than the one imposed by the AUC.

[9] We have taken a notational liberty in order to simplify the presentation. $P_{A/B}(\beta) \doteq P_A(\beta)$ iff β is a reflexive or reciprocal; otherwise β is a pronoun and $P_{A/B}(\beta) \doteq P_B(\beta)$.

agreement is irrelevant. Lemma 1, while still mathematically correct, is correspondingly no longer relevant to human language. What then is the complexity of the Anaphora Problem under the empirically-superior Anaphoric Uniqueness Condition?

According to the AUC, two anaphoric elements can share an antecedent only if each independently agrees with that antecedent. Therefore, the Anaphora Problem under the AUC is equivalent to the problem of finding at least one available antecedent for every anaphoric form attested in a given input utterance. Once we have found an available antecedent for each attested anaphoric form, we may link each occurance of that anaphoric form to its available antecedent without violating the AUC.

LEMMA 2 Anaphoric Uniqueness is $O(n^2)$.

Proof 2 The input consists of a paradigm $P = \langle P_A, P_B \rangle$ for anaphoric elements and an utterance containing the 3-tuple $A = \langle A^A, A^B, A^C \rangle$ of disjoint sets of arguments. On such an input, the following simple algorithm decides in time $O(|P| \cdot |A|)$ whether or not there is a linking for A that does not violate the AUC.

First we create a singly-linked list of the anaphoric forms in P that are attested in A. Let this list, of length less than $\min\{|P|, |A^C|\}$, be called the *attested list*. For each available antecedent $r_i \in A^C$, we calculate the unique reflexive form $P_A(r_i)$ that agrees with r_i and the unique pronoun form $P_B(r_i)$ that agrees with r_i. In the worst case, we may be required to examine nearly the entire labeling function in P, which would require time $O(|P|)$.

Next, we determine whether $P_A(r_i) \in A^A$ and whether $P_B(r_i) \in A^B$. This requires constant time if we store the anaphoric elements $A^A \cup A^B$ in a hash table. If $P_A(r_i) \in A^A$, then we are assured that every instance of $P_A(r_i)$ in A^A can be assigned an antecedent (namely r_i) without violating the AUC. Therefore, we remove $P_A(r_i)$ from the attested list, also in constant time. Likewise, if $P_B(r_i) \in A^B$, then we remove $P_B(r_i)$ from the attested list. If at any point during this procedure the attested list becomes empty, then we halt and accept because every anaphoric element in the input may find an available antecedent that it agrees with. On the other hand, if the attested list is not empty after we have iterated over every $r_i \in A^C$, then we halt and reject because the anaphoric elements remaining in the attested list do not agree with any available antecedent.

There are $O(|A|)$ available antecedents, each of which may be processed in time proportional to the size $|P|$ of the paradigm structure. Therefore, the algorithm requires time $O(|P| \cdot |A|)$, or $O(n^2)$ for an input of size n. □

This decision procedure may be converted into a constructive algorithm for the Anaphoric Uniqueness Problem as follows. When we find the anaphoric elements $P(r_i)$ that agree with r_i in $A^A \cup A^B$, we simply add the relation $\mathsf{link}(\alpha, r_i)$ for each $\alpha \in P(r_i)$ to a list of potential links. If any anaphoric element in A^A or A^B does not have a potential link to some reference when we have finished iterating over the references, then we halt and reject. Otherwise, we output an actual linking, by selecting exactly one potential link for each anaphoric element in $A^A \cup A^B$, and then halt. It does not matter which potential link is chosen: although different choices will result in different antecedence relations, and therefore different intepretations), every choice will satisfy the AUC and correspond to a possible interpretation.

The paradigm structure P of anaphoric forms and the preference function Υ are superficially similar. Both restrict the possible antecedents of anaphoric elements in a manner that is relatively easy to satisfy. However, there are crucial differences between the two. The paradigm structure models the relatively static linguistic information available to the language user, while the preference function models the continually-changing extralinguistic information available to the language user. The unitary language computation is able to output infinitely many linkings that violate the preference function, but is entirely unable to output even a single linking that violates the paradigm structure. The class of possible paradigm structures is also more constraining than the class of possible preference functions: every logically possible linking is consistent with some fixed preference function, but there exist many logically possible linkings that are not consistent with any fixed paradigm structure.

This concludes the minimizer's turn in the language complexity game for anaphora. In this section we considered the SAC and the AUC, both narrow models of the linguistic information available to the language user. In the next section, we model a considerable amount of the linguistic information available to the language user, including information about phrase structure and about referential dependencies such as the relations of obviation and immediate antecedence. In our role as maximizer in the language complexity game for anaphora, we would like to prove that the Anaphora Problem is more complex than previously thought. We cannot use the standard agreement condition of section 3.1, because it has just been falsified by the minimizer. Nor can we use the anaphoric uniqueness condition of section 3.3, because it has just been shown polynomial time. The goal of the next chapter, then, is to find some way to reduce an NP-complete problem to the problem of computing the antecedence relations in a way that satisfies the obviation relations.

4 Referential Dependency

We have seen that anaphoric elements must have antecedents, subject to an agreement condition, perhaps the anaphoric uniqueness condition. A second component of linguistic knowledge is that that pronouns must be disjoint in reference from certain linguistic arguments. For example, every English speaker knows that *Todd hurt him* cannot normally mean that 'Todd hurt Todd'. This judgement of disjoint reference, that the pronoun *him* cannot refer to the argument *Todd*, is depicted here by assigning *him* the subscript of *Todd*, preceded by an asterisk.

The prohibition against sharing referential values is enforced globally, as shown by the examples in (15).

(15) a. John$_1$ said that [Bill$_2$ liked him$_{1/*2}$].
  b. John$_1$ said that [he$_{1/*2}$ liked Bill$_2$].
  c. *John$_1$ said that [he$_1$ liked him$_1$].

The object *him* can refer to *John* in (15a); the embedded subject *he* can refer to *John* in (15b); but *he* and *him* cannot both refer to *John* in (15c), because *he* and *him* are obligatorily disjoint in reference.

For the same reasons that knowledge of coreference must be represented in the language user, and hence by every scientifically adequate linguistic theory, so must knowledge of disjoint reference. In particular, we are led to postulate a second abstract linguistic relation: an intransitive, symmetric, irreflexive obviate(α, β) relation that holds between two linguistic elements α and β that cannot share any referential values [16, 40].

Every linguistic representation therefore includes a set of A of arguments, a symmetric obviate relation O, $O \subset A \times A$, and an asymmetric link relation L, $L \subset A \times A$. We represent the obviate and link relations by a graph $G = \langle A, O, L \rangle$ of referential dependencies whose undirected edges obviate$(a_1, a_2) \in O$ represent the obligatory nonoverlapping reference of the arguments a_1 and a_2, and whose directed edges link(e, a) $\in L$ represent that the argument a is the immediate antecedent of the anaphoric element e. This graph is called the Referential Dependencies Graph (RDG).

The Anaphora Problem in this model of referential dependencies ("Referential Dependencies") is defined as follows. The input consists of a linguistic representation R lacking relations of referential dependency but containing the 3-tuple $\langle A^A, A^B, A^C \rangle$ of disjoint sets of arguments, where A^A consists of reflexives and reciprocals, A^B consists of pronouns, and

A^C consists of referring-expressions. As above, A^C is the set of available antecedents, while $A \doteq A^A \cup A^B \cup A^C$ is the universe of linguistic arguments in the representation R. The output is a correct referential dependency graph $G = \langle A, O, L \rangle$ that is compatible with R. The corresponding decision problem is to decide whether or not there exists a correct RDG compatible with the representation R.

The goal of this chapter is to model the linguistic information that determines link and obviate relations. In section 4.1, the maximizer proposes a model based primarily on the work of Chomsky [16, 18], Higginbotham [39, 40], and Lasnik [59, 60, 61]. This referential dependency model specifies a mapping from certain configurations in a linguistic representation to certain relations of referential dependency. In section 4.2, we prove that the anaphora problem is NP-hard according this model.

4.1 The Referential Dependence Model

What then is the exact relation between a linguistic representation R and its graph G of referential dependencies?

First, the referential dependency graph G must be correct in and of itself. Every anaphoric element in G must have an immediate antecedent, and two anaphoric elements cannot share any antecedents if they are obviative. This is illustrated in (15c), where the two pronouns *he* and *him* are obviative and hence only one of the two pronouns can have the subject *John* as its antecedent. Recall that link$^+$ is the positive transitive closure of the assymetric link relation. Then an RDG $G = \langle A, O, L \rangle$ is *correct* if and only if (i) every anaphoric element α, $\alpha \in (A^A \cup A^B)$, is linked to some immediate antecedent β, $\beta \in A$; and (ii) link$^+(\alpha_1, \beta)$ $\in L^+$ and link$^+(\alpha_2, \beta) \in L^+$ only if obviate$(\alpha_1, \alpha_2) \notin O$. This definition of correctness does not provide for the poorly-understood phenomenon of split antecedence. To mitigate this minor empirical deficiency, the proof of lemma 3 below only makes use of singular pronouns, which do not give rise to split antecedents in any human language.[1]

Second, the linguistic representation R and its referential dependency

---

[1]To include split antecedents in our definition of the Anaphora Problem, we might restate clause (ii) to require obviative anaphoric elements to have at least one distinct antecedent β, as in "obviate$(\alpha_1, \alpha_2) \Rightarrow \exists \beta \in A$ [link$^+(\alpha_1, \beta) \in L^+$ and link$^+(\alpha_2, \beta) \notin L^+$]." However, this definition is not entirely correct because, as shown in examples (16), obviation is not always enforced when a pronoun has split antecedents.

graph G must be compatible. They must be defined on the same set of arguments A and certain configurations in R must give rise to particular referential dependencies in G. For example, when a pronoun is the direct object of a verb, then it must obviate the subject of that verb, as illustrated in (15a,c) for the embedded verb *like*.

In the remainder of this section we consider exactly how configurations in R are mapped into subgraphs of G. To do this, we examine the distribution of link and obviate relations in a range of syntactic configurations. The result of our investigation will be an inventory of primitive correspondences between linguistic representations and their referential dependency graphs. We will use these primitive correspondences to construct increasingly complex referential dependency graphs with the property that each is compatible with a possible linguistic representation (by construction), yet a significant amount of computation is needed to determine if these RDGs are also correct. Let us begin constructing our inventory of primitive correspondences.

4.1.1 Local c-command Configuration

We say α *c-commands* β in a phrase structure tree if and only if all branching nodes that dominate α in the tree also dominate β.[2] In particular, the direct object of a verb c-commands the verb's indirect object, and the subject c-commands both direct and indirect objects. To a first approximation, we say two elements are *local* if they are co-arguments, that is, thematic arguments of the same verb or noun. As we shall see,

---

(16) a. John$_1$ suggested to Bill$_2$ that [he$_2$ shoot them$_{\{1,2\}}$].
 b. John$_1$ reminded Kate$_2$ that [he$_1$ introduced them$_{\{1,2\}}$ to the Pope].

The subject and direct object of a verb are obviative. Therefore, we incorrectly expect *he* and *them* to not share any referential values in (16a,b). The examples in (17) suggest that lexical factors, such as the choice of verb, play a surprisingly significant role.

(17) a. Navarre$_1$ suggested to Benedict$_2$ that [he$_2$ persuade them$_{i=\{1,2\}}$]
  [PRO$_i$ to perjure themselves$_i$]].
 b. *Navarre$_1$ suggested to Benedict$_2$ that [he$_2$ tell them$_{i=\{1,2\}}$]
  [PRO$_i$ to perjure themselves$_i$]].

Although obviation is enforced in (17b) but not in (17a), the only overt difference between the two examples is the choice of the embedded verb (*persuade* versus *tell*).

[2] A phrase structure tree is a hierarchical representation of the syntactic phrases assigned to expressions. Examples of such phrases include verb phrase (VP), noun phrase (NP), and sentence (S). Alternately, a phrase structure tree is a derivation tree for an expression of a formal language according to the formal grammar of that language. See [111, ch.28], or [43, ch.4.3] for examples and introductory discussion.

the exact definition of local c-command does not matter for our purposes: all that matters here is the fact that antecedence and disjoint reference are understood to be possible or necessary in some configurations, and not in others.

The first syntactic configuration with consequences for referential dependencies is local c-command: reflexives (and reciprocals) must link to some locally c-commanding β, and pronouns must obviate all such β. In addition, each anaphoric element obviates all referring-expressions that it c-commands, regardless of whether they are local or not, as illustrated in example (20) below. (In the linguistics literature, the requirement that reflexives and reciprocals have local antecedents is binding condition A, the requirement that pronouns be locally obviative is binding condition B, and the third requirement, that referring-expressions not be the antecedent of any c-commanding anaphoric element, is binding condition C. Collectively, these conditions are called the binding theory.)

A reflexive must be linked to a unique local c-commanding element. This is illustrated by the paradigm in (18), where the domain of locality is indicated by square brackets.

(18) a. [John$_1$ shot himself$_1$]
   b. [John$_1$ introduced Bill$_2$ to himself$_{1/2}$]
   c. John$_1$ thought Bill$_2$ said [Mary liked himself$_{*1/*2}$]

Example (18b) shows that a reflexive in the indirect object position can take any c-commanding antecedent inside its local domain; example (18c) shows that a reflexive must have some antecedent inside its local domain. *Mary* is not a possible antecedent for *himself* in (18c) because they disagree on gender.

Pronouns are locally obviative: a pronoun cannot share referential values with any linguistic element that c-commands it in its local domain. The domain of locality is roughly — although not exactly — the same as for reflexives. (Again, all is needed for our complexity analysis below is that there exist configurations that result in obviation.) This is illustrated by the paradigm in (19).

(19) a. [John$_1$ shot him$_{*1}$]
   b. [John$_1$ introduced Bill$_2$ to him$_{*1/*2}$]
   c. John$_1$ thought Bill$_2$ said [Mary liked him$_{1/2}$]

Example (19b) shows that a pronoun is disjoint from all locally c-commanding elements; example (19c) shows that a pronoun can link to any element outside its local domain.

Pronouns (and other anaphoric elements) also obviate all referring-expressions that they c-command, regardless of whether they are local or not. This is illustrated in (20).

(20) a. [He$_{*1}$ shot John$_1$]
  b. [He$_{*1/*2}$ introduced John$_1$ to Bill$_2$]
  c. Mark told himself$_{*1/*2/*3/*4}$ that [he$_{*1/*2/*3/*4}$ said that [John$_1$ thought [Bill$_2$ wanted [Sam$_3$ to like Fred$_4$]]]]

Obviation applies equally to all linguistic coreference, including the intra- and inter-sentential linking of pronouns, because obviation cannot be violated, even if a pronoun and its antecedent are in different sentences. Without loss of generality then, all linkings in this chapter will be intra- or inter-sentential, according to convenience.[3]

The other local c-command configuration is "exceptional case-marking" (ECM). Certain verbs are exceptional case-marking because, unlike verbs that take a finite clausal complement, ECM verbs take an infinitival clausal complement and assign abstract case to its subject. Common ECM verbs in English include *want, expect, believe, prefer*, and semantically related verbs.

In an ECM configuration, the subject of an ECM verb locally c-commands the subject of its infinitival complement. This is illustrated by the paradigm in (21), with the ECM verbs *want* and *expect*.

(21) a. John$_1$ wants [himself$_1$ to shoot Bill]
  b. John$_1$ expects [him$_{*1}$ to shoot Bill]

---

[3]Pronouns may also find their antecedents extra-linguistically in (at least) two ways, neither of which prejudices our discussion. First, the antecedent of a pronoun may be 'demonstrated' extra-linguistically, as when the speaker points to an antecedent seen by the hearer. For example, if a speaker were to say *Bill saw HIS mother* while stressing the pronoun and vigorously pointing to Jack, then the hearer might understand *HIS* to extra-linguistically refer to "Jack." Second, a pronoun may have no antecedent available, in which case it becomes necessary for the hearer to postulate some new, heretofore unmentioned, mental referent without a prior linguistic antecedent. For example, if we are warned to "Watch out for him," we must postulate the existence of some male individual M that we must watch out for. If we are then told "he's coming to get you," we would relate the subject pronoun *he* to the previously postulated individual M. There appears to be a significant cognitive cost to this invention of unmentioned antecedents, because language users are reluctant to do so.

Examples (21) demonstrate that the subject *John* of an ECM verb locally c-commands the subject α of the infinitival complement [α *to shoot Bill*], for both reflexives and pronouns.

Our goal as maximizer is to prove that the Anaphora Problem is NP-hard, without using any agreement constraints. Our underlying idea is to reduce an NP-complete problem to the problem of computing the antecedence relations in a way that satisfies the obviation relations. Let us briefly pause to consider how such a reduction might work.

Imagine that we must color the following four-vertex graph

$$G_4 = \{(1,2), (2,3), (3,4), (4,2)\}$$

using three colors. Then our reduction might construct a sentence containing three available antecedents and four pronouns. The first part of the sentence, *Before Mark$_a$, Phil$_b$, and Hal$_c$ were friends....*, would represent the three colors, where each proper noun corresponds to a different color. The second part of the sentence would have an obviation graph equivalent to G_4, where the pronoun p$_i$ in the sentence corresponds to vertex i in G_4. As expected, it is difficult to understand the resulting sentence (22).

(22) Before Mark$_a$, Phil$_b$, and Hal$_c$ were friends,
   [he$_1$ wanted him$_2$ to introduce him$_3$ to him$_4$].

The obviation graph for (22) is shown in (23).

(23)

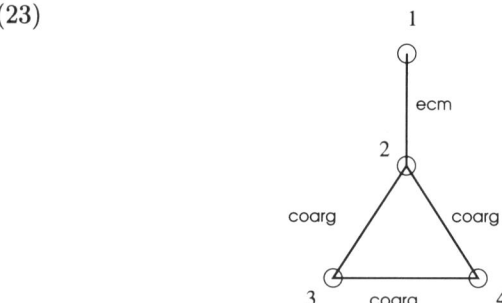

Each vertex in the obviation graph (23) is labeled with the numerical index of its corresponding pronoun, and each edge is labeled with the syntactic configuration responsible for the corresponding **obviate** relation. (Briefly, "**coarg**" means "argument of same verb or noun," and "**ecm**" means "exceptional case-marking configuration.")

By carefully grounding the reference of each pronoun in turn, the English speaker can confirm that the obviation graph for (22) exactly corresponds to the four-vertex graph G_4. Let he_1 link to $Mark_a$ in the sentence—this corresponds to coloring vertex 1 in G_4 with the color a. Then in the simplified sentence [$Mark$ wanted him_2 to introduce him_3 to him_4], the English speaker will note that $Mark$ can be the antecedent of any pronoun but him_2 — this corresponds to G_4, where coloring vertex 1 with a given color only prevents us from coloring vertex 2 the same color. Continuing in this fashion, the English speaker may convince himself that the pronouns in such a sentence can find their antecedents in the sentence if and only if the corresponding graph G_4 is 3-colorable.

The local c-command configurations used in (22) only give rise to simple obviation graphs that are easily colored. Therefore, in our role as maximizer, we must extend the referential dependence model to include three additional syntactic configurations: control, strong crossover, and invisible obviation.

4.1.2 Control Configuration

In the expression *Sarah screamed before jumping*, all English speakers know that *Sarah* is the understood subject of the gerund *jumping*, that is, everyone knows that Sarah did the jumping. In order to represent this linguistic knowledge — as we must — we may postulate a silent pronoun 'PRO' in the subject position of the adjunct [*before jumping*], and obligatorily link the silent subject pronoun to *Sarah*, as depicted in (24).

(24) Sarah$_1$ screamed [before PRO$_1$ jumping]

This is called "subject control" because the reference of PRO is controlled by the subject of the main clause.

Further evidence for the existence of this silent pronoun comes from its interaction with overt anaphoric elements. Observe that *himself* must refer to *Mark* in (25a), and *him* must be disjoint from *Mark* in (25b).

(25) a. Mark$_1$ vomited [after PRO$_1$ getting himself$_1$ plastered]
    b. Mark$_1$ vomited [after PRO$_1$ getting him$_{*1}$ plastered]

Without PRO, such facts are a complete mystery. But once the understood subject of the gerund is explicitly represented using PRO, as we have done in (25), the facts are trivially accounted for as canonical configurations of local c-command between silent PRO and an overt anaphoric element.

In any event, our complexity analysis will proceed whether silent pronouns exist or not: all that matters for our complexity analysis is the empirical fact that *himself* must refer to *Mark* in utterances such as (25a), and that *him* must be disjoint from *Mark* in (25b).

Another example of subject control appears in (26a) with the verb *promise*. Contrast this to the verb *persuade* in (26b), which is an object control verb.

(26) a. Tom$_1$ promised Mary$_2$ [PRO$_{1/*2}$ to attend school]
    b. Tom$_1$ persuaded Mary$_2$ [PRO$_{*1/2}$ to attend school]

The meaning of (26a) is that "Tom promised Mary that he, Tom, would attend school," while (26b) means that "Tom persuaded Mary that she, Mary, would attend school." PRO is used here to represent the invisible, understood subject α of the embedded clause [α *to attend school*].

4.1.3 Strong Crossover Configuration

"Wh-movement" is the configuration involving a wh-phrase, such as [*who*] or [*what person*], that appears displaced from its underlying position as an argument of a verb or other thematic function. A *trace* is used to mark the underlying position of such a displaced argument. For example, in *Who$_k$ did Mary see t_k*, the underlying position of the wh-phrase *who$_k$* as the direct object of the verb *see* has been marked with a trace t_k coindexed with the wh-phrase *who$_k$*. This represents the fact that *who$_k$* stands in the same relation to the verb *see* as it does in the related utterance *Mary saw who*.

"Strong crossover" occurs when an anaphoric element α intervenes between a wh-phrase and its trace, and c-commands the trace. In such a configuration, α obviates the subject of the wh-phrase. This is shown in (27a), where the pronoun *he* c-commands the trace t_k of the wh-phrase [*which person*], and for this reason must be understood as disjoint from the person who Mary kissed.

(27) a. [Which person]$_k$ did he$_{*k}$ say t_k kissed Mary.
    b. [Which person]$_k$ t_k said he$_k$ kissed Mary.

In (27b), however, there is no strong crossover configuration, and no obviation. That is, (27b) has an interpretation of the form: "for which person x, did x say x kissed Mary?" Although we need not postulate any traces for the purposes of our complexity analysis below, such facts are difficult to explain without an explicit trace, because the wh-phrase [*which person*] and the pronoun *he* stand in the same structural relation in both sentences.

In the utterance *The man who$_k$ Mary saw t_k*, we say that *who* heads the relative clause [*who Mary saw*], and that *who* predicates [*the man*], its subject. When the relative clause contains a pronoun in a strong crossover configuration, then the pronoun obviates the subject of the relative clause, as in (28).

(28) [the man]$_1$ [who$_k$ he$_{*1}$ likes t_k].

4.1.4 Invisible Obviation Configuration

"Ellipsis" is the syntactic phenomenon where a phrase is understood but not expressed in words, as in *The men ate dinner and the women did too*, which can only be understood to mean that 'the women did eat dinner too'. For this example, we would say that the verb phrase [$_{VP}$ *eat dinner*] has been ellipsed in the second conjunct; this is called VP-ellipsis.

Recall from section 3.3 above that anaphoric elements in an ellipsed VP can give rise to invariant and covariant readings, as shown in (29).

(29) Felix$_1$ [hates his$_1$ neighbors] and so does Max$_2$ [e].
([*hate his$_{1/2}$ neighbors*])

In each example, careful attention must be paid to the relevant construal of the null structure, indicated with square brackets, and the intended reference of anaphoric elements, as indicated in the italicized parenthetical following the example.

Briefly, a configuration of "invisible obviation" arises in a coordinated structure between the arguments of the overt verb phrase in the first conjunct and the subject of an ellipsed verb phrase in the second conjunct, because the subject of the ellipsed verb phrase in effect locally c-commands the overt verb phrase and its overt arguments. For example, *him* can refer to *Mark* in (30a), but not in (30b).

(30) a. Jesse$_1$ likes him$_2$ and Mark$_2$ likes her$_1$.
   b. Jesse$_1$ likes him$_{*2}$ and Mark$_2$ does [e] too.

In (30b) the subject of the ellipsed VP (the proper noun *Mark*) invisibly obviates the overt direct object (the pronoun *him*), because they are in an invisible configuration of local c-command.

The fact that the utterance (30b) is assigned a referential dependencies graph where *him* obviates *Mark* is all that is required for our subsequent complexity analyses. However, to the best of our knowledge the phenomenon of invisible obviation has not hitherto been discussed in the published linguistics literature, and therefore it will benefit our understanding of human language to examine the phenomenon of invisible obviation in greater detail.

A referring-expression is invisibly obviative from its local c-commanders, as in (31), where pragmatic considerations strongly favor a coreferential interpretation that can only be excluded by syntactic principles.

(31) Aphrodite likes Narcissus$_1$ and he$_{*1}$ does [e] too.

Coreference becomes possible with heavy contrastive stress on *he*, but this fact is not relevant here, in part because heavy contrastive stress often suffices to overcome overt binding condition C violations as well.[4]

There are a number of subtleties, however, the most interesting of which is that invisible obviation is entirely a local phenomena, as illustrated in (34).

(34) a. He$_{*1}$ knew Juliet loved Romeo$_1$.
   b. The nurse [knew Juliet loved Romeo$_1$] before he$_1$ did [e].
      ([*know Juliet loved Romeo$_1$*])

---

[4]In general, it appears that both overt and invisible condition C effects between two R-expressions can be overcome with heavy phonological stress, as in (32), whereas invisible condition C effects between an R-expression and a c-commanding pronoun are inviolable, regardless of the amount of stress (33).

(32) a. BILL$_1$ wanted BILL$_1$ to kiss Mary.
   b. Sue [wanted BILL$_1$ to kiss Mary] and BILL$_1$ did [e] too.

(33) a. * He/HE$_1$ wanted Bill/BILL$_1$ to kiss Mary.
   b. * Sue [wanted Bill/BILL$_1$ to kiss Mary] and he/HE$_1$ did [e] too.

Although the pronoun *he* must be obviative from the R-expression *Romeo* that it overtly c-commands in (34a), it need not be obviative from the R-expression that it invisibly c-commands in (34b).

In fact, the domain of invisible obviation is exactly the local domain of binding condition B. We capture this observation with the *Invisible Obviation Condition* (IOC), which states that a pronoun or R-expression α contained in the overt antecedent of an ellipsed phrase invisibly obviates an overt element β if and only if, after ellipsed phrases are hypothetically reconstructed from their overt antecedents, a pronoun γ in the reconstructed position of α would obviate β. Although the IOC is somewhat cumbersome to state, the idea is simple and is illustrated schematically in figure 4.1, and by means of an example in (35).

In (35a), *him* invisibly obviates *John* because after the ellipsed verb phrase [e] is reconstructed from its overt antecedent [*likes him*] in (35b), a pronoun γ in the position of the reconstructed direct object would obviate *John*.

(35) a. Kate [likes him] and John does [e] too.
   b. ... and John$_1$ does [like γ_{*1}] too.

The IOC is a descriptive generalization that follows from deeper linguistic principles, as discussed in chapter 5. We illustrate the IOC with examples for both pronouns (36b,37b) and R-expressions (36c,37c):[5]

(36) a. Bill$_1$ wanted him$_{*1}$ to kiss Mary.
   b. Sue [wanted him$_{*1}$ to kiss Mary] and Bill$_1$ did [e] too.
   c. Sue [wanted Bill$_1$ to kiss Mary] and he$_{*1}$ did [e] too.

(37) a. Bill$_1$ wants PRO$_1$ to love him$_{*1}$.
   b. Sue wants Mary to [love him$_{*1}$] and Bill$_1$ wants PRO$_1$ to [e] (too).
   c. Sue wants him$_1$ to [love Mary] and Bill$_1$ wants PRO$_1$ to [e] (too).

Examples (38) demonstrate that the nonlocal obviation defined by binding condition C is not relevant to the IOC.

---

[5] The examples in (36b) and (37b) are constructed using a unique antecedent *Bill* to more clearly reveal the invisible obviation configuration. However, the IOC appears to overlap in these examples with an independent (and not entirely understood) constraint that excludes some cross-conjunct antecedences, as in *Bill wanted him$_{*1}$ to win and Tom$_1$ wanted himself to win (too)*.

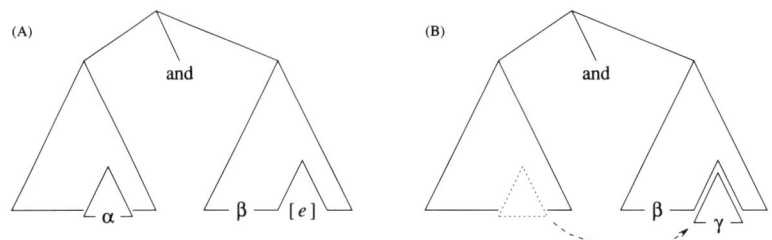

Figure 4.1
A schematic illustration of the Invisible Obviation Condition (IOC). The linguistic representation depicted in (A) consists of two conjuncts. The second conjunct contains an overt argument β and an ellipsed phrase $[e]$ whose antecedent is in the first conjunct. The first conjunct contains an overt argument α, either a pronoun or a referring-expression, that is contained in the antecedent of the ellipsed phrase. The IOC states that α and β are invisibly obviative in (A) if and only if β and a pronoun γ would be obviative in the hypothetical representation (B). That is, α and β are invisibly obviative in (A) if and only if a pronoun γ in the reconstructed position of α would obviate β after the ellipsed phrase $[e]$ is hypothetically reconstructed from its overt antecendent, as shown in (B). The dashed arrow depicts the hypothetical reconstruction of the ellipsed phrase $[e]$ in the second conjunct from its overt antecedent $[\ldots \alpha \ldots]$ in the first conjunct.

(38) a. $Bill_1$ wanted Mary to kiss him_1.
   b. He_{*1} wanted Mary to kiss $Bill_1$.
   c. Sue [wanted Mary to kiss him_1] and $Bill_1$ did $[e]$ too.
   d. Sue [wanted Mary to kiss $Bill_1$] and he_1 did $[e]$ too.

The fact that the IOC should be defined relative to binding condition B and not in terms of (the negation of) binding condition A is illustrated with a prepositional adjunct in (39), and with a possessive NP in (40).

(39) a. $Bill_1$ saw a snake near him_1/$himself_1$.
   b. He_{*1} saw a snake near $Bill_1$.
   c. Tom [saw a snake near $Bill_1$] before he_1 did $[e]$.

(40) a. $Bill_1$ knew that pictures of him_1/$himself_1$ would be on sale.
   b. He_{*1} knew that pictures of $Bill_1$ would be on sale.
   c. Sue [knew that pictures of $Bill_1$ would be on sale] before he_1 did $[e]$.

The elliptical structure is not an invisible pronoun, simply because there is no invisible obviation when an overt pronoun is used (41b) instead of ellipsis (41a).

(41) a. Juliet$_1$ thought that the Friar$_2$ [poisoned her$_1$] without realizing she$_{*1}$ did [e].
  b. Juliet$_1$ thought the Friar$_2$ [poisoned her$_1$]$_3$ without realizing that she$_1$ did it$_3$.

If the null structure were simply an empty pronoun, then there would be no way to explain the lack of invisible obviation in (41b).

The following examples are particularly interesting because they demonstrate that local obviation in the overt structure is preserved in the null structure, even when it is embedded one level, as in (42), or more than one level, as in (43).

(42) a. Bill$_i$ [wants PRO$_i$ to love him$_{*i}$].
  b. Sue$_i$ [wants PRO$_i$ to love Bill$_1$] and he$_{*1}$ does [e] too.
  c. Sue$_i$ [wants PRO$_i$ to love him$_{*1}$] and Bill$_1$ does [e] too.

(43) a. Bill$_i$ [expects PRO$_i$ to want PRO$_i$ to love him$_{*i}$].
  b. Sue$_i$ [expects PRO$_i$ to want PRO$_i$ to love Bill$_1$] and he$_{*1}$ does [e] too.
  c. Sue$_i$ [expects PRO$_i$ to want PRO$_i$ to love him$_{*1}$] and Bill$_1$ does [e] too.

Contrast these examples to the examples (44), which show that the nonlocal obviation of binding condition C is not similarly preserved under embedding.

(44) a. Bill$_i$ [wants PRO$_i$ to know if Mary loves him$_i$].
  b. He$_i$ [wants PRO$_i$ to know if Mary loves Bill$_1$]. ($i \neq 1$)
  c. Sue$_i$ [wants PRO$_i$ to know if Mary loves Bill$_1$] and he$_1$ does [e] too.
  d. Sue$_i$ [wants PRO$_i$ to know if Mary loves him$_1$] and Bill$_1$ does [e] too.

These facts are exactly in accordance with the IOC.[6]

Finally, consider the discourse (46) and its variant (47).

---

[6]Chomsky [18] and other authors have tried to explain strong crossover phenomenon as arising from binding condition C. The fact that so-called "condition C effects" do not arise in elliptical structures gives us a direct empirical test for this hypothesis. The facts of invisible strong crossover in (45) refute the hypothesis that strong crossover is due to binding condition C.

(45) a. The man who$_i$ Mary$_1$ said that he$_{*i}$ likes t_i.
  b. The man who$_i$ he$_{*i}$ said that Mary$_1$ likes t_i.
  c. The man who$_i$ Mary$_1$ [said that she$_1$ likes t_i] and who$_i$ he$_{*i}$ did [e] too.

(46)
Ann: Romeo$_1$ wants Rosaline$_2$ to [love him$_1$].
Ben: Not any more—now Romeo$_1$ wants Juliet$_3$ to [e].
([love him$_1$])

(47)
Ann: Romeo$_1$ wants Rosaline$_2$ to [love him$_i$]. ($i = 1$)
Ben: Not any more—now Rosaline$_2$ wants Romeo$_1$ to [e].
([love him$_i$], $i \neq 1$)

In both examples, Ann's use of the pronoun *him* is most naturally understood as referring to *Romeo*. Yet when Ben replies in example (47), the English speaker will be thrown in a state of confusion because the coreferential interpretation ($i = 1$) is no longer possible in Ann's statement.

This invisible relation of local obviation can also be created entirely within a sentence (48), with the pronoun understood as first including but later obviating the subject *Romeo*.

(48)
Romeo$_1$ wanted Rosaline$_2$ to [love him$_i$] before wanting himself$_1$ to [e].

The referential dependency graph (RDG) for (48) is depicted in (49):

(49)

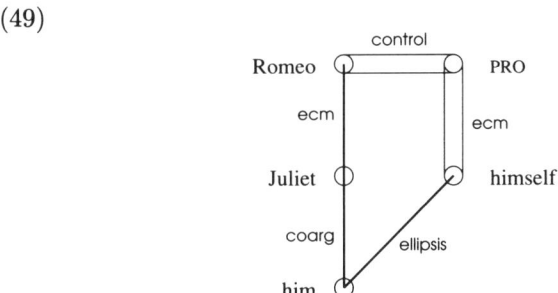

As summarized by the IOC, binding condition C does not apply in full to elliptical contexts: an overt pronoun in the subject position of an ellipsed VP does not obviate the nonlocally c-commanded ellipsed elements of that ellipsed VP. Therefore, if strong crossover was in fact due to binding condition C, then the pronoun *he* in subject position of the ellipsed VP [e] would not obviate the ellipsed wh-trace t_i that it nonlocally c-commands in (45c) and no crossover phenomena would arise, contrary to observed fact.

Single lines depict relations of obviation, while double lines depict relations of coreference. The double lines are intended to suggest the coalescing of coreferential arguments in the RDG. Vertices are labeled with the corresponding noun phrase arguments, and the edges are labeled with the configurations to which they are attributable.

In short, two elements α and β are invisibly obviative in an overt utterance if and only if a pronoun γ obviates β in a hypothetical utterance that is constructed by first replacing α with γ and then replacing each ellipsed phrase with its overt antecedent (as illustrated in figure 4.1). This concludes our brief digression into the nature of invisible obviation.

We have just seen how our linguistic analysis is simplified by the use of abstract relations, such as obviate and link, and nonovert elements, such as traces and PRO. Therefore, we should rationally include these relations and elements in our language model.

However, it is important to realize that the complexity classifications of this chapter do not depend on the existence of empty elements (such as traces and PRO) or abstract linguistic relations (such as c-command, exceptional case-marking, control, and wh-movement), or on any other detail of our linguistic analysis. The complexity analysis below (in particular, the proof of lemma 3) relies only on empirical facts of anaphoric interpetation — that an overt anaphoric element must corefer or be disjoint in reference from certain other overt elements in certain attested utterances — and that these empirical facts generalize in a reasonable manner. The proof of lemma 3 below may be straightforwardly adapted to the E-language perspective, to prove the NP-hardness of the problem of recognizing the set of sentences with the property that every anaphoric element in the sentence may find its antecedent in that sentence in a manner that concords with human judgments of coreference and disjoint reference. The linguistic analysis is included to advance our understanding of human language and to state the empirical generalization to unbounded utterances, when the facts of referential interpretation are more difficult to elicit.

This concludes our survey of the language user's knowledge of referential dependence. The result of our investigation is an inventory of primitive correspondences between a linguistic representation R and its referential dependency graph G, that describe how certain configurations in R are mapped into subgraphs of G. The next step is a complexity analysis of the Anaphora Problem under this referential dependencies model.

4.2 From Satisfiability to Referential Dependence

As suggested above in examples (22,23), the conceptually natural reduction is from the graph coloring problem to the Anaphora Problem under the referential dependencies model. However, the transformation of arbitrary graphs into obviation relations is cumbersome and nontrivial. To overcome this difficulty, our reduction will be from 3SAT to Referential Dependencies.

In order to study relations of referential dependency in complete isolation from the agreement properties of anaphoric elements, we will require all anaphoric elements to have the same inflectional features (in particular, all anaphoric elements will be third person masculine singular).

LEMMA 3 3SAT $\leq_\mathcal{P}$ Referential Dependencies.

Proof 3 On input a Boolean formula f consisting of the clauses $C = \{C_1, C_2, \ldots, C_p\}$ in the Boolean variables $X = \{x_1, x_2, \ldots, x_n\}$, our reduction ρ outputs a possible linguistic representation $\rho(f) = R$ lacking only relations of referential dependency such that there exists a correct referential dependency graph $G = \langle A, O, L \rangle$ that is compatible with R iff the formula f is satisfiable. The linguistic representation $\rho(f) = R$ is shown schematically in figure 4.2.

The idea of the reduction is to map the components of a Boolean formula f into the components of a linguistic representation $\rho(f)$. In particular, ρ will map truth values into available antecedents (that is, referring-expressions), literals into pronouns, and truth assignments to variables into antecedence relations from the pronouns to the available antecedents. The mapping is performed in such a transparent manner that the assignment of a truth value v to a variable x_j would exactly correspond to the linking of the pronoun $\rho(x_j)$ to the antecedent $\rho(v)$ and the linking of the pronoun $\rho(\overline{x}_j)$ to the antecedent $\rho(\neg v)$.

It is not enough to simply map the components of a formula f into the components of a representation $\rho(f) = R$. The mapping must also preserve the semantics of f. The reduction outputs a representation R such that there exists a correct RDG compatible with R if and only if f is satisfiable. The formula f is satisfiable if and only if there exists a truth assignment to the variables such that every 3-clause in f contains at least one true literal. Accordingly, ρ will map global truth assignments into correct RDGs, and satisfied 3-clauses into compatible RDGs. Without loss of generality, let $C_i = (a_i \vee b_i \vee c_i)$ be the ith 3-clause in the formula f. Then the mapping will ensure that at least one of the pronouns $\rho(a_i)$, $\rho(b_i)$, or $\rho(c_i)$ is linked to the antecedent $\rho(\text{'true'})$ in every correct RDG compatible with R. Let us now turn to the details of how this is accomplished.

The linguistic arguments A in the representation R are partitioned into three disjoint sets according to their referential properties: reflexives and reciprocals are in A^A; pronouns are in A^B; and R-expressions are in A^C. The set A^C is the set of all available antecedents; it contains exactly three distinct antecedents: *True*, *False*, and *Neutral*. These noun phrases represent, respectively, the truth value 'true', the truth value 'false', and the absence of an assigned truth value. The set A^B will contain two pronouns for every Boolean variable x_j, one to represent its positive literals (x_j) and the other to represent its negative literals $(\bar{x}_j)$. In order to preserve the semantics of negation, these pronouns must obviate each other. Both will also obviate the proper noun *Neutral*, and therefore can only link to the antecedents *True* or *False*. To accomplish this, our reduction builds the object control construction $\rho(x_j)$ shown in figure 4.3, that contains two possible antecedents for VP-ellipsis, VP(x_j) and VP$(\bar{x}_j)$.

The pronoun him_j in figure 4.3 is the direct object of its own verb phrase VP(x_j), and therefore him_j will invisibly obviate the overt subject of any ellipsed VP whose antecedent is VP(x_j). The same is true of the pronoun him_{*j} and the verb phrase VP$(\bar{x}_j)$. As shown in figure 4.4, our reduction takes advantage of this by mapping each positive literal of x_j into an ellipsed VPs $[e]_{x_j}$ whose antecedent is VP(x_j), and mapping each negative literal of x_j into an ellipsed VP $[e]_{\bar{x}_j}$ whose antecedent is VP$(\bar{x}_j)$.

Finally, for each Boolean 3-clause $C_i = (a_i \vee b_i \vee c_i)$, the reduction outputs the rather intricate syntactic structure $\rho(C_i)$ shown in figure 4.4. Figure 4.5 shows the minimal referential dependency graph $G_i = \langle A_i, O_i, L_i \rangle$ that is compatible with $\rho(C_i)$. That is, a correct RDG $G = \langle A, O, L \rangle$ is compatible with $\rho(C_i)$ if and only if $A = A_i$, $O = O_i$, and $L \supset L_i$. The effect of the referential dependency graph G_i in combination with the limited number of available antecedents A^C is to ensure that one of the three ellipsed verb phrases in figure 4.4 must have as its antecedent an overt verb phrase from an object control construction of figure 4.3 that contains a pronoun linked to the antecedent *True*. This corresponds exactly the requirement that each Boolean 3-clause contain a true literal. This concludes our reduction from 3SAT. □

It is of course not to be expected that the linguistic expressions constructed by the preceding reduction are easy to comprehend. Nor is this fact relevant here. Recall that our goal is to illuminate the structure and complexity of language computations, not to characterize the arbitrary limits of our finite abilities.

The proof of lemma 4 in section 5.2 below can easily be adapted to give a second NP-hardness proof for the Anaphoric Preference Problem in the referential dependency model, where each pronoun is no more than four-ways ambiguous, and no agreement features or configurations of invisible obviation are used.

All that remains is to state the main theorem of this section.

THEOREM 1 The Anaphora Problem is NP-hard.

Proof 4 By lemma 3, and the NP-completeness of 3SAT. □

We now have a complexity lower-bound for human language computations that relies only on the empirical facts of referential dependency, and on the uncontroverted assumption that these facts generalize in a reasonable manner. It does not matter exactly how the conditions on coreference and disjoint reference are stated, only that there are such conditions, as there are in all known human languages. Therefore, we expect that this NP-hardness result applies to all adequate linguistic theories, and that it is true of human language itself. Moreover, the directness of the reduction suggests that the Anaphora Problem is one of the more difficult subproblems of language comprehension, because graph coloring is one of the most difficult NP-complete problems, with no known polynomial-time approximation scheme.

In the next chapter, we expand our language model for the Anaphora Problem to include ellipsis. Continuing in our role as maximizer in the language complexity game for anaphora, we propose a model of ellipsis that is based on a widely-accepted generative theory of ellipsis. We prove that the Anaphora Problem is PSPACE-hard under this copy model of ellipsis. The minimizer's turn follows. In the role of minimizer, we show that the copy model of ellipsis is empirically flawed and propose an

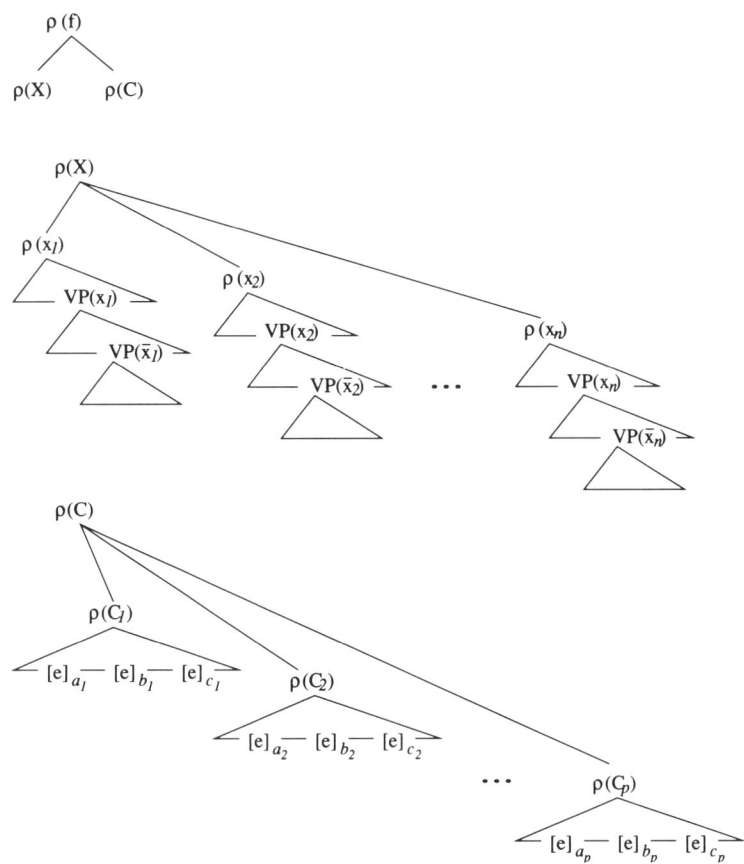

Figure 4.2
On input the Boolean formula f, our reduction ρ outputs the linguistic representation $\rho(f) = R$ lacking only relations of referential dependency, as shown schematically. The Boolean formula f consists of the clauses $C = \{C_1, C_2, \ldots, C_p\}$ in the Boolean variables $X = \{x_1, x_2, \ldots, x_n\}$. For each Boolean variable x_j, our reduction outputs the linguistic representation $\rho(x_j)$, an object control construction containing two verb phrases, $\text{VP}(x_j)$ and $\text{VP}(\bar{x}_j)$, that are potential antecedents of VP-ellipsis. The linguistic representation $\rho(x_j)$ is shown in figure 4.3. For each Boolean 3-clause $C_i = (a_i \vee b_i \vee c_i)$, our reduction outputs the linguistic representation $\rho(C_i)$ shown in figure 4.4. The construction $\rho(C_i)$ contains three ellipsed VPs — $[e]_{a_i}$, $[e]_{b_i}$, and $[e]_{c_i}$ — whose antecedents are from the object control constructions on the left of this figure. Without loss of generality, let a_i be a negative literal of the variable x_j. Then the overt verb phrase $\text{VP}(\bar{x}_j)$ in the construction $\rho(x_j)$ is the antecedent of the ellipsed verb phrase $[e]_{a_i}$ and the pronoun him_{*j} in $\rho(x_j)$ invisibly obviates NP_6, the overt subject of the ellipsed VP $[e]_{a_i}$ in $\rho(C_i)$.

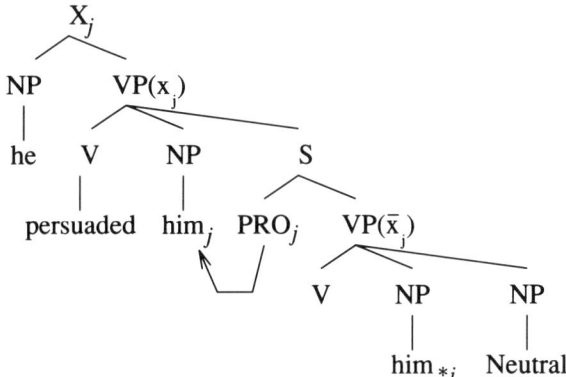

Figure 4.3
The Boolean variable x_j is mapped into the linguistic representation $\rho(x_j)$, an object control construction that contains two possible antecedents for VP-ellipsis, $\text{VP}(x_j)$ and $\text{VP}(\bar{x}_j)$. In this construction, PRO_j locally c-commands the pronoun him_{*j} for $\bar{x}_j$ in the lower clause, and so they are obviative (by binding condition B). Moreover, both PRO_j and the pronoun him_{*j} for $\bar{x}_j$ c-command the referring-expression *Neutral*, and therefore both must obviate it (by binding condition C). The object control verb *persuade* obligatorily links PRO_j to the pronoun him_j for x_j, as depicted by the arrow. The subject position of *persuade* is filled with a "dummy" pronoun *he* so as not to increase the number of available antecedents A^C in the construction. In any RDG compatible with $\rho(x_j)$, the pronoun him_j must refer to either *True* or *False*, the pronoun him_{*j} must refer to the other of the two antecedents, and neither pronoun can refer to *Neutral*. In short, this representation ensures consistency of truth assignments, as well as correctly representing the semantics of Boolean negation. As shown in figure 4.4, a positive literal of x_j will be mapped into ellipsed VP whose antecedent is $\text{VP}(x_j)$, while a negative literal of x_j will be mapped into an ellipsed VP whose antecedent is $\text{VP}(\bar{x}_j)$. This is the representation that would be assigned to utterances such as *He persuaded him to introduce him to Hector*.

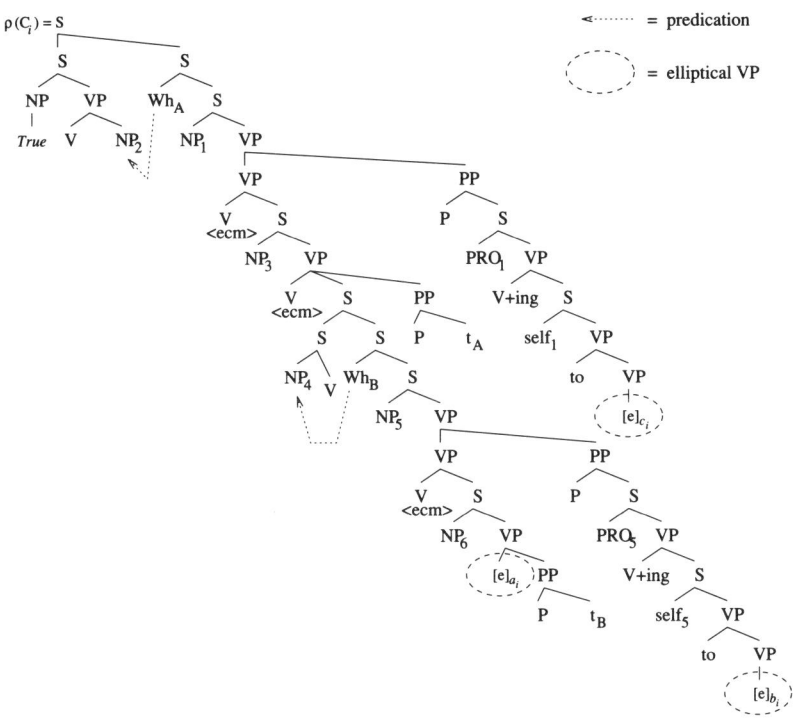

Figure 4.4
The Boolean 3-clause $C_i = (a_i \vee b_i \vee c_i)$ is mapped into the linguistic representation $\rho(C_i)$, which contains configurations of local c-command, strong crossover, adjunct control, and invisible obviation. "S" is a sentential clause, "NP" is a noun phrase, "VP" is a verb phrase, and "PP" a prepositional phrase. All NPs dominate pronouns, which are not shown for reasons of clarity. Dashed arrows depict the predication of a noun phrase by an extraposed relative clause. Figure 4.5 shows the the minimal referential dependencies graph G_i that is compatible with the representation $\rho(C_i)$. That is, any correct RDG compatible with $\rho(C_i)$ must have exactly the same vertices and obviation relations as G_i, and must contain all link relations in G_i. Each of the ellipsed VPs ($[e]_{a_i}$, $[e]_{b_i}$, and $[e]_{c_i}$) refers to one of the overt VPs in the n control constructions, as described above in figure 4.2. Consequently, NP_6 and the pronoun that represents the literal a_i are in a relation of invisible obviation, as are NP_5 and the pronoun for b_i, and NP_1 and the pronoun for c_i. These obviation relations are shown in figure 4.5. This representation would be assigned to natural utterances such as *True met him$_2$, who$_A$ he$_1$ expected him$_3$ to want him$_4$ framed, who$_B$ he$_5$ believed he$_6$ did [e] with t_B after exposing himself$_5$ to [e] for t_A, before telling himself$_1$ to [e]*. Indices, traces of wh-movement, and elliptical VPs ("[e]") are included in the expression to help the reader align the expression with its representation.

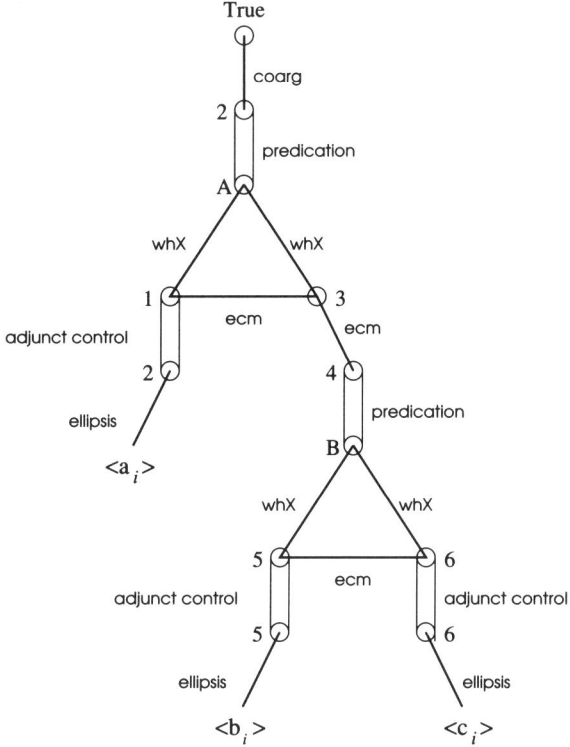

Figure 4.5
This is the minimal referential dependency graph G_i compatible with the linguistic representation $\rho(C_i)$ of figure 4.4. That is, any correct RDG compatible with $\rho(C_i)$ must have exactly the same vertices and obviation relations as G_i, and must include all link relations in G_i. As above, single lines depict obviation relations and double lines depict relations of coreference, such as links and predications. Vertices in the RDG correspond to noun phrase arguments, and are labeled with the identifying indices from figure 4.4. The vertices $\langle a_i \rangle$ $\langle b_i \rangle$, and and $\langle b_i \rangle$ are the direct objects of the overt VPs in figure 4.3 that are the antecedents of the ellipsed VPs $[e]_{a_i}$, $[e]_{b_i}$, and $[e]_{c_i}$ in figure 4.4. The edges in this referential dependency graph are likewise labeled with the configurations to which they are attributable. Recall that "**coarg**" and "**ecm**" are configurations of local c-command; "**whX**" is for a strong crossover involving a wh-phrase; and "**ellipsis**" for the invisible obviation arising from the ellipsis of a verb phrase representing the relevant Boolean literal from figure 4.3. The obviation graph that results when coreferential vertices are coalesced, in combination with the three available antecedents A^C, ensures that at least one of "invisible" pronouns — each of which is the direct object of an ellipsed VP — must link to the proper noun *True* in any correct RDG compatible with the representation $\rho(C_i)$. This corresponds exactly to the constraint that a true Boolean 3-clause contain at least one true literal.

improved model of ellipsis, called the sharing model. Finally, we prove that the Anaphora Problem is NP-complete according to the sharing model.

5 Ellipsis

This chapter extends the language complexity game for anaphora into a new empirical domain, that of syntactic ellipsis. In order to comprehend an utterance containing ellipsed material, the language user must in effect "reconstruct" the ellipsed material in that utterance and compute the antecedents of any anaphoric elements in the reconstructed material. Failing that, the language user has failed to completely comprehend the utterance. This is the broad computational problem posed by ellipsed anaphoric elements in human language comprehension.

For example, in order to comprehend the English utterance *Joey did his homework and but Steven didn't*, the language user might determine that the verb phrase *do his homework* has been ellipsed from the second conjunct, and that therefore the utterance has the meaning '$Joey_1$ did his_1 homework but $Steven_2$ didn't *do his_2 homework*,' where $Joey_1$ is the intended antecedent of the overt pronoun *his* in the first conjunct, and $Steven_2$ is the intended antecedent of the ellipsed pronoun *his* in the second conjunct.

Let us begin with some terminology to clarify our discussion of ellipsis. Let R be a linguistic representation containing two coordinated structures, S and S', where S' contains ellipsed material ϵ_i whose overt antecedent X_i is contained in the structure S. Then we say two overt elements β and β' *correspond* in R if and only if β is in S, β' is in S', and β and X_i stand in the same relation to each other in the structure S as β' and ϵ_i do in the structure S'. In example (50), *Felix* and *Max* correspond, as do *Kyle* and *Lester*.

(50) a. Felix [hates his neighbors] and so does Max [e].
b. Felix told Kyle [that he hates his neighbors]
  and Max told Lester [e].

In example (50a), *Max* is the subject of an ellipsed verb phrase [e] whose antecedent is the verb phrase [*hates his neighbors*], which has *Felix* as its subject. In example (50b), *Max* is the subject of a verb whose indirect argument is an ellipsed clause [e] whose antecedent [*that he hates his neighbors*] is the indirect argument of a verb that has *Felix* as its subject.

In this chapter, we construct two precise and increasingly realistic models of the Anaphora Problem with ellipsis and analyze their computational complexities. In the first model, ellipsis is seen as the literal reconstruction of ellipsed material. In the second model, ellipsis is seen as the reapplication of a pre-existing thematic function. Both models are informed by the work of Reinhart [79], Sag [91], and Williams [107].

Our technical results may be summarized as follows. In section 5.1, the maximizer presents the copy model of ellipsis, and motivates it with well-known empirical arguments from generative linguistics. The copy model accounts for basic facts of ellipsed anaphora, for example, that the utterance *Felix hates his neighbors and so does Max* in (50a) is ambiguous between an "invariant" interpretation where Max hates Felix's neighbors and a "covariant" interpretation where Max hates his own neighbors. Next, in section 5.2, the maximizer proves that the Anaphoric Preference Problem is PSPACE-hard under this copy model of ellipsis.

With the insight gained from the complexity analysis, the minimizer confronts the copy model with linguistic counterexamples in section 5.3 and proposes an improved function-sharing model of ellipsis in section 5.4. The function-sharing model explains the interaction between ellipsis and anaphora in terms of the thematic structure of utterances. In particular, the function-sharing model represents ellipsed material as a second application of a prexisting thematic function. Finally, in section 5.5, the minimizer proves that the Anaphoric Preference Problem is contained in $\mathcal{NP}$ under this function-sharing model of ellipsis. By reducing the complexity of the Anaphoric Preference Problem in elliptical structures to inside $\mathcal{NP}$, while strictly improving the empirical adequacy of our language model, these rounds of the language complexity game provide evidence for an $\mathcal{NP}$ upper bound on the complexity of the Anaphora Problem (with and without the preference function).

5.1 Copy Model of Ellipsis

Let us begin at the beginning. We have seen that language users understand elliptical structures as though they really exist. That is, language users know both the location of the ellipsed material, as shown in (51a), and its content, as shown in (51b).

(51) a. The men ate dinner and the women did [e] too.

b. 'the men ate dinner and the women did [*eat dinner*] too'.

These facts about linguistic knowledge must be represented in the language user, and therefore by any plausible model of language. One representation of the language user's knowledge of ellipsis — arguably the most straightforward one — consists of two parts. First, the location of the ellipsed material is identifed with a null element, which may be depicted "$[e]$," as in (51a). Let us call this representation of the overt properties of an utterance its *surface representation*. Next, the content of the ellipsed material is "reconstructed" into the location of the ellipsed material, by simply copying the overt material into the location of the ellipsed material, as first suggested by Chomsky [13]. Let us call this representation of the language user's knowledge of utterances the *underlying representation*.[1]

An elliptical structure may itself be understood as containing an elliptical structure, as in (52a), which is understood to mean (52b).

(52) a. Jack [[corrected his spelling mistakes]$_1$ before the teacher did $[e]_1]_2$ and Ted did $[e]_2$ too.
b. Jack corrected his spelling mistakes before the teacher did *correct his spelling mistakes* and Ted did *correct his spelling mistakes before the teacher did correct his spelling mistakes*.

This suggests that the copying operation that defines the underlying representation of an elliptical utterance is recursive. The depth of its recursion does not appear to be constrained by the principles of grammar, as shown in (53).

(53) Harry [claims that Jack [[corrected his spelling mistakes]$_1$ before the teacher did $[e]_1]_2$ and that Ted did $[e]_2$ too]$_3$, but Bob doesn't $[e]_3$.

The elliptical structure behaves as though it was really there. In section 4.1.4, we saw that the subject of an ellipsed VP can obviate the direct obect of an overt VP that it does not c-command, as in (54).

(54) a. Jesse$_1$ likes him$_{*2}$ and Mark$_2$ does $[e]$ too.
b. Aphrodite likes Narcissus$_1$ and he$_{*1}$ does $[e]$ too.

These facts are not readily explained by the standard binding conditions, and require special treatment in our model of referential dependency (section 4.1). However, if the content of the ellipsed material is indeed

---

[1] In much of the generative linguistics literature, our underlying representation of elliptical utterances is included in the so-called logical form of an utterance, along with the graph of referential dependencies.

copied to the location of the ellipsed material, then the disjoint reference facts illustrated in (54) are straightforwardly reduced to a configuration of local c-command between the overt subject of the ellipsed VP and the direct object of the copied VP in the underlying representation, as shown in (55).

(55) a. ... and Mark$_2$ does [like him$_{*2}$] too.
   b. ... and he$_{*1}$ does [like Narcissus$_1$] too.

The ellipsed structure is not merely a silent VP-pronoun, simply because the obviation violation in (56a) vanishes when an overt VP-pronoun is used instead in (56b).

(56) a. Juliet$_1$ thought the Friar$_2$ [poisoned her$_1$] without realizing that she$_{*1}$ did [e].
   b. Juliet$_1$ thought the Friar$_2$ [poisoned her$_1$]$_3$ without realizing that she$_1$ did it$_3$.

In our discussion of anaphoric agreement in section 3.3, we observed that an anaphoric element in the overt structure and its copy in the ellipsed structures may be understood as having different antecedents, as in (57), where the invisible pronoun *his* is ambiguous, referring either to *Felix* in (57a) ('invariant' interpretation) or *Max* in (57b) ('covariant' interpretation).

(57) a. Felix$_1$ [hates his$_1$ neighbors] and so does Max$_2$ [e].
       ([hate his$_1$ neighbors])
   b. Felix$_1$ [hates his$_1$ neighbors] and so does Max$_2$ [e].
       ([hate his$_2$ neighbors])

This suggests that an anaphoric element may be linked to its antecedent either *before* the overt structure is copied, resulting in the invariant interpretation (58), or *after* copying, resulting in the covariant interpretation (59).

(58) a. Felix$_1$ [hates his$_1$ neighbors] and so does Max$_2$ [e].
   b. Felix$_1$ [hates his$_1$ neighbors] and so does Max$_2$ [hate his$_1$ neighbors].

(59) a. Felix$_1$ [hates his neighbors] and so does Max$_2$ [e].
   b. Felix$_1$ [hates his$_1$ neighbors] and so does Max$_2$ [hate his$_2$ neighbors].

Recall that the ellipsed pronoun must agree with its overt antecedent, which excludes the covariant interpretations in (60) that are possible in the minimally different examples in (61).

(60) a. Barbara$_1$ read her$_1$ book and Eric$_2$ did [e] too.
     ([read her$_{1/*2}$ book])
   b. You$_1$ ate your$_1$ vegetables and so did Bob$_2$ [e].
     ([eat your$_{1/*2}$ vegetables])

(61) a. Barbara$_1$ read her$_1$ book and Kate$_2$ did [e] too.
     ([read her$_{1/2}$ book])
   b. You$_1$ ate your$_1$ vegetables and so did you$_2$ [e].
     ([eat your$_{1/2}$ vegetables])

The covariant interpretation is forced when the antecedent of the anaphoric element is a quantified noun phrase (QNP), as shown in (62).

(62) Every man$_1$ [ate his$_1$ dinner] and so did every boy$_2$ [e]
     ([eat his$_{*1/2}$ dinner])

That is, (62) must mean that every boy ate his own dinner; it cannot mean that every boy ate every man's dinner. Therefore, an anaphoric element α must be linked to its immediate antecedent β in the underlying representation when β is a quantified noun phrase (that is, α must link to β after copying).

In short, there is significant evidence that the content of the overt antecedent of an ellipsed structure must be copied to the location of the ellipsed structure in the underlying representation. We also saw that this copying is a recursive process, and that anaphoric elements may be linked to their antecedents either before or after the copying, and that they must be linked after copying when their antecedent is a quantified noun phrase.

These observations are formalized in the *copy model of ellipsis*, which states that: (i) the underlying representation of an utterance is constructed by (recursively) copying the overt material into the position of the corresponding ellipsed material; (ii) an anaphoric element α may link to its antecedent either before or after copying; (iii) an anaphoric element must agree with its antecedent after copying, according to the paradigm structure for anaphoric forms; and (iv) when the antecedent of α is a quantified NP β, then α must link to β after copying.[2] The copy model also includes the referential dependency model, which maps configurations in the underlying representation into obligatory relations of obviation and immediate antecedence. Although we have included the anaphoric uniqueness condition in the copy model (iii), our lower bound proof below does make use of it.

The Anaphoric Preference Problem in this copy model ("Anaphoric Copying") is the problem of computing the referential dependencies of the underlying representation in a manner that respects the preference function. The input consists of a preference function Υ and a surface representation R lacking only relations of referential dependency, where R contains the 3-tuple $\langle A^A, A^B, A^C \rangle$ of disjoint sets of arguments. As above, A^A consists of reflexives and reciprocals, A^B of pronouns, and A^C of referring-expressions. A^C is the set of available antecedents, while $A \doteq A^A \cup A^B \cup A^C$ is the universe of linguistic arguments in the representation R. In addition, the location of all ellipsed structures and their overt antecedents are marked in R. The output is a correct referential dependency graph $G = \langle A', O, L \rangle$ with the maximally-preferred linking L that is compatible with the underlying representation R' corresponding to the surface representation R. The related decision problem is to decide whether or not there exists a correct RDG G with preference value at least $p_{\min}$ that is compatible with the underlying representation R' corresponding to R.

A complexity result depends only on the input-output mapping specified by a computational problem; it does not depend on how that mapping is specified. Therefore, any language model that agrees with the copy model on whether or not certain elliptical utterances can be assigned correct referential dependencies will also inherit the computational complexity of the copy model. That is, any language model that represents the meaning of anaphora in elliptical utterances using devices that can achieve the effect of the copy operation will inherit the computational complexity of our copy model. This is true regardless of how that language model is defined, how many levels of representation it has,

---

[2]The first account of invariant and covariant interpretations in VP ellipsis, due to Ross [90], is equivalent to this copy model, because deletion in Ross's deep-structure to surface-structure derivation is identical to copying in the mapping from surface representation to underlying representation. This copy model has been recently (re)proposed in the linguistics literature by Kitagawa [53], and is often assumed by other linguists in passing (cf. [54, 70, 74]).

or what they are called.

5.2 From QBF to Anaphoric Copying

On the one hand, the copy model appears to possess tremendous computational power because it performs recursive copying. If the language user must in fact repeatedly copy overt material to the location of ellipsed material in order to interpret the anaphoric elements in the ellipsed material, then the task of comprehending ellipsed anaphoric elements can quickly require an infeasible amount of computational space.

On the other hand, the Anaphoric Copying Problem is a decision problem that requires only a Yes/No output. Therefore, it does not explicitly require recursive copying. An algorithm for this problem need not output the underlying representation of an utterance, or even output a correct RDG compatible with the underlying representation of that utterance. Rather, it need only determine whether or not there exists a correct referential dependency graph compatible with the underlying representation. Therefore, the complexity of the Anaphoric Copying Problem hinges on the exact relationship between the surface representation of an utterance and the RDG of the corresponding underlying representation.

If this relationship is complex, then the Anaphoric Copying Problem is complex. But if this relationship is simple, then the Anaphoric Copying Problem is also simple. If, for example, we can prove that the existence of a correct RDG compatible with a given surface representation also implies the existence of a correct RDG compatible with the corresponding underlying representation, then the Anaphoric Copying Problem trivially reduces to the Referential Dependency Problem, and syntactic ellipsis does not add any extra computational complexity to the Anaphora Problem.

Before presenting our complexity analysis, we would like to stress once more that this research monograph only considers the problem of computing linguistic representations, which is a trivial subproblem of the much more intractable and less well understood problem of determining the 'truth' or 'truth conditions' of a given utterance. The following proof shows that calculating the referential dependencies of a particular class of utterances can be as difficult as determining the truth of quantified

Boolean formulas. As discussed in chapter 2, the proof does *not* make the entirely trivial and nugatory argument that determining the 'truth' or 'truth conditions' of the utterances of a human language language can be as difficult as determining the truth of quantified Boolean formulas described by means of natural language utterances.

LEMMA 4 Quantified 3SAT $\leq_\mathcal{P}$ Anaphoric Copying.

Proof 5 The input to our reduction ρ is a quantified Boolean formula Ω in prenex 3-CNF, consisting of alternating quantifiers
$\forall x_1 \exists x_2 \ldots \forall x_{n-1} \exists x_n$
preceding (and quantifying the literals in) the clauses
$C = C_1, C_2, \ldots, C_p$
in the Boolean variables $X = x_1, x_2, \ldots, x_n$. Each clause contains exactly three distinct literals labeled by
$C_i = (a_i \lor b_i \lor c_i)$.

On such an input Ω, our reduction ρ outputs a binary-valued preference function Υ, a minimum preference value $p_{\min}$, and a surface representation $\rho(\Omega) = R$ lacking only relations of referential dependency such that Ω is true if and only if there exists a correct referential dependency graph $G = \langle A', O, L \rangle$ with preference value $\Upsilon(L) \geq p_{\min}$ that is also compatible with the underlying representation R' corresponding to R. The linguistic representation $\rho(\Omega) = R$ is shown schematically in figure 5.1. The reduction does not rely on the agreement properties of anaphoric elements, and therefore, it holds for *any* model of anaphoric agreement, even one without agreement features.

As in the proof of lemma 3, the idea of the reduction is to map the components of the QBF Ω into linguistic "gadgets" that together make up the linguistic representation $\rho(\Omega) = R$. Conceptually, the reduction maps quantifiers into available antecedents (that is, R-expressions), literals into pronouns, and the quantification of variables in Ω into the linking of pronouns in R'. The difficulty of the reduction lies in designing the linguistic gadgets to have the properties needed to ensure the correctness of the reduction.

It is helpful to think of the QBF Ω as sequence of Boolean predicates in one quantified variable, that is, $\Omega = \forall x_1 P_1(x_1)$, $P_1(x_1) = \exists x_2 P_2(x_1, x_2)$, and so on. Then our reduction will map each quantifier Qx_i in Ω into a linguistic gadget that contains a pair of available antecedents, one to represent the truth assignment $x_i = 0$ and the other to represent $x_i = 1$. A universally quantified predicate $\forall x_i P(x_i)$ in Ω is mapped into an ellipsis gadget: a VP-ellipsis structure whose two corresponding subjects are the available antecedents representing the truth assignments $x_i = 0$ and $x_i = 1$, whose overt verb phrase represents the predicate $P(x_i = 0)$ in R', and whose ellipsed verb phrase represents the predicate $P(x_i = 1)$ in R'. An existentially quantified predicate $\exists x_{i+1} P(x_{i+1})$ is mapped into a strong crossover gadget: a linguistic structure whose RDG ensures that all pronouns that link to one of its two available antecedents must link to the same antecedent (either the antecedent representing $x_{i+1} = 0$, or the antecedent representing $x_{i+1} = 1$).

Each Boolean 3-clause C_j is mapped into a pigeonhole gadget: a configuration $\rho(C_j)$ in R that contains three pronouns, one for each literal in C_j, plus two available antecedents. These two antecedents are preferred by each of the three pronouns (and by no other anaphoric elements in R), and so each pronoun in R prefers a total of exactly three antecedents. The representation $\rho(C_j)$ results in obviation relations that require at least one of three pronouns to link to its preferred antecedent outside of $\rho(C_j)$, in some $\rho(Qx)$. Positive literals of the variable x_i are mapped into pronouns that prefer the antecedent representing $x_i = 1$, while negative literals of x_i are mapped into pronouns that prefer the antecedent representing $x_i = 0$. This has the effect of ensuring that every copy of $\rho(C_j)$ in the underlying representation R' has a correct preferred RDG if and only if C_j contains a true literal in every quantifier-determined truth assignment.

The reduction is performed in two conceptual stages. In the first stage, the quantifiers of Ω are mapped into components of R one by one, from outside in. In the second stage, the 3-clauses of Ω are mapped into components of R, in no particular order.

The reduction maps a universally quantified predicate
$\forall x_i P_i(x_1 = v_1, x_2 = v_2, \ldots, x_i)$
into a VP-ellipsis structure in R. Recall that a universally quantified predicate $\forall x_i P_i(x_i)$ is true if and only if $P_i(x_i = 0)$ is true and $P_i(x_i = 1)$ is true. The latter Boolean conjunction can be expressed in a VP-ellipsis construction whose surface representation is abstracted in (63).

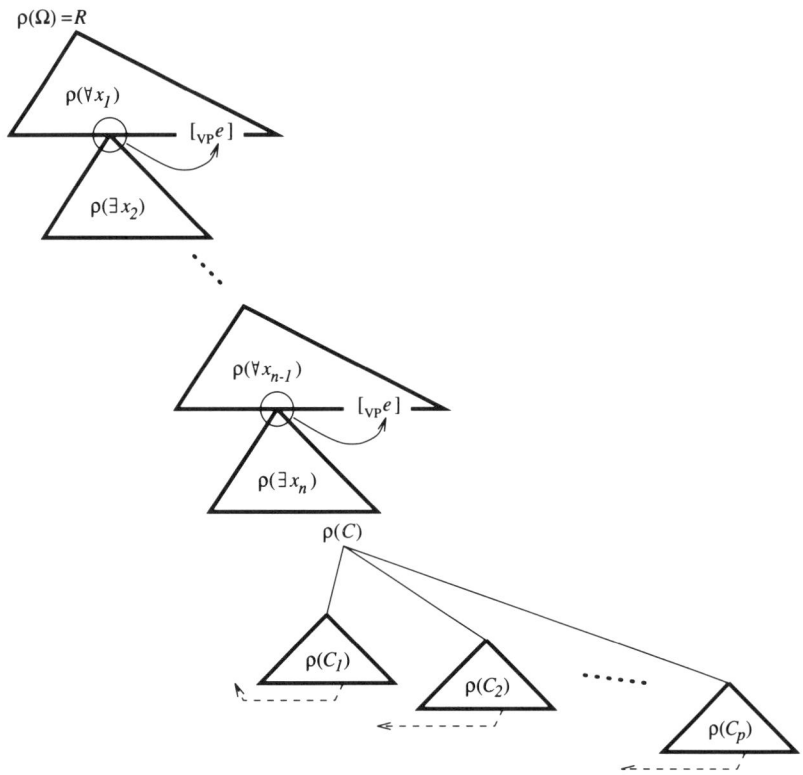

Figure 5.1
The surface representation $R = \rho(\Omega)$ that corresponds to the input instance $\Omega = \forall x_1 \exists x_2 \ldots \forall x_{n-1} \exists x_n [C_1, C_2, \ldots C_p]$. Each quantifier Q over the Boolean variable x_i is mapped into a structure containing two available antecedents, to represent the two possible truth assignments to the quantified variable x_i. Each universal quantifier $\forall x_i$ is mapped into an ellipsis gadget. In the underlying representation corresponding to R, each of the $n/2$ circled overt VPs is copied to its corresponding ellipsed VP position [$_{VP}e$], according to the copy model. Each existential quantifier $\exists x_{i+1}$ is mapped into a strong crossover gadget, as discussed in the text. Each 3-clause C_j is mapped into a pigeonhole gadget that contains three pronouns, one for each literal in C_j. One of these three pronouns (the *selected* pronoun) must link to an antecedent outside that construction, in some dominating ellipsis or strong crossover gadget. These obligatory long distance links are drawn with dashed arrows. Each selected pronoun corresponds to the literal that satisfies a given 3-clause.

Ellipsis

(63)

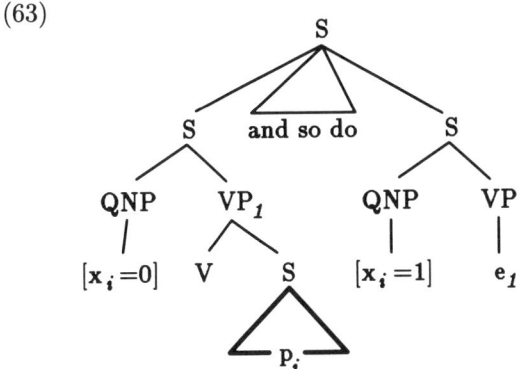

According to the copy theory, the language user represents the ellipsis construction (63) in the abstracted underlying representation (64). First, the overt VP is copied to the position of the ellipsed VP. Next, pronouns inside the original and copied VPs link to one of their preferred antecedents independently.

(64)

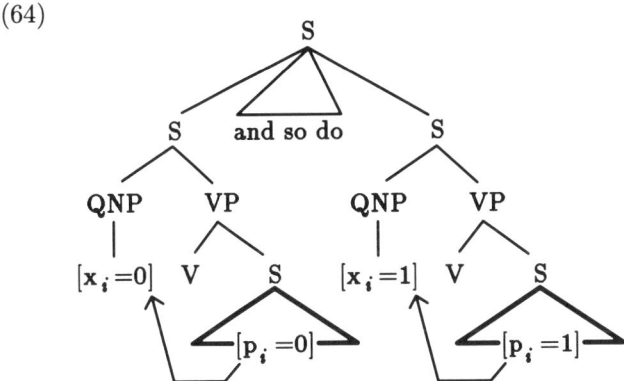

The overt VP in the surface representation represents the Boolean predicate $P_i(x_i)$; the pronoun p_i contained in this overt VP represents a true literal of x_i inside $P_i(x_i)$; the two QNP subjects are available antecedents that represent the truth assignments $x_i = 0$ and $x_i = 1$, respectively. Each pronoun p_i must link to the subject of its own conjunct in the underlying representation, because the subjects are quantified noun phrases. Therefore the pronoun p_i in the first (overt) VP may only link to the first subject [$_{\text{QNP}}$ $x_i = 0$], which represents the conjunct $P_i(x_i = 0)$, and the copied pronoun p_i in the second (copied) VP may only link to the second subject [$_{\text{QNP}}$ $x_i = 1$], which represents the conjunct $P_i(x_i = 1)$.

As shown in figure 5.1 above, the verb phrase will also contain the construction (65) that represents the existential quantifier $\exists x_{i+1}$.

The reduction maps an existentially quantified predicate
$\exists x_{i+1} P_i(x_1 = v_1, x_2 = v_2, \ldots, x_{i+1})$
into a strong crossover configuration in R. An existentially quantified predicate $\exists x_{i+1} P(x_{i+1})$ is true if and only if $P(x_{i+1} = 0)$ is true or $P(x_{i+1} = 1)$ is true. This Boolean disjunction can be expressed in a construction whose surface representation is (65).

(65)

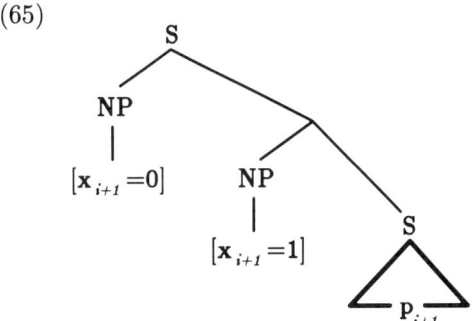

This structure will have two possible interpretations, as represented by the two underlying representations in (66):

(66)

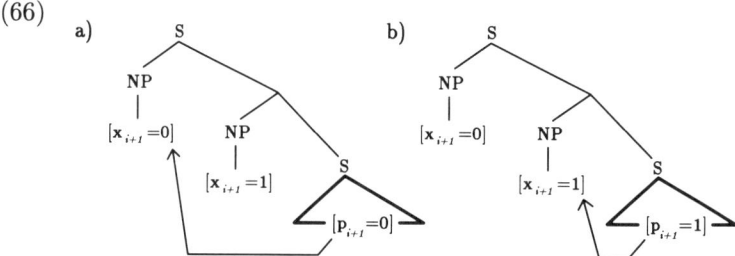

The embedded clause represents the predicate $P_{i+1}(x_{i+1})$; the pronoun p_{i+1} represent a true literal of x_{i+1} inside the predicate $P_{i+1}(x_{i+1})$; the two NPs are available antecedents that represent the truth assignments $x_{i+1} = 0$ and $x_{i+1} = 1$, respectively. According to the preference function Υ, p_{i+1} prefers these two noun phrases. However, linguistic constraints disclosed below ensure that p_{i+1} can link to the first NP

[NP $x_{i+1} = 0$] if and only if $P_{i+1}(x_{i+1} = 0)$ is true, as shown in (66a); and that p_{i+1} can link to the second NP [NP $x_{i+1} = 1$] if and only if $P_{i+1}(x_{i+1} = 1)$ is true, as shown in (66b).

The embedded clause will also contain the construction (63) that represents the next quantifier $\forall x_{i+2}$, as shown in figure 5.1 above.

The requirement that the Boolean literals in C must receive consistent truth assignments is mapped into the requirement that all embedded pronouns representing true literals of x_{i+1} must link to the same antecedent. This constraint may be enforced using the powerful strong crossover configuration introduced above in section 4.1. The details of how this might be done arose from discussions with Alec Marantz, who suggested all the examples.

Recall that strong crossover is the configuration where an anaphoric element c-commands the trace of a displaced wh-phrase and intervenes between the wh-phrase and its trace as well. In such a configuration, the anaphoric element obviates the subject of the wh-phrase.

(67) a. Who$_k$ did he$_{*k}$ say Mary kissed t_k.
  b. [the man]$_1$ [who$_k$ he$_{*1}$ likes t_k].

The noun phrase in (67b) contains a relative clause [*who he likes t*] that predicates [*the man*]; the pronoun *he* is in a strong crossover configuration, and therefore cannot refer to [*the man*], which is the subject of the relative clause.

Now consider the effect of extraposing a relative clause containing a strong crossover configuration in (68).

(68) a. At the airport, a man$_1$ met Jane$_2$,
  who$_{k=1/*2}$ she$_2$ likes t_k.
  b. At the airport, a man$_1$ met Jane$_2$,
  who$_{k=*1/2}$ he$_1$ likes t_k.

In (68a), if we understand *she* as referring to *Jane*, then we must understand *who* as predicating *a man*. Conversely, if we understand *he* as referring to *a man* in (68b), then *who* must predicate *Jane*. This simple example establishes the ambiguity of predication when the predicate is an extraposed relative clause containing a strong crossover configuration.

When the extraposed relative clause contains two obviative pronouns, as in (69), then the sentences cannot have the intended interpretation because the relative clause must predicate some subject, yet cannot without violating strong crossover.

(69) a. *At the airport, [a man]$_1$ met Jane$_2$,
    who$_k$ she$_2$ thinks he$_1$ likes t_k.
 b. *At the airport, [a man]$_1$ met Jane$_2$,
    who$_k$ he$_1$ thinks she$_2$ likes t_k.

This example establishes that the strong crossover configuration gives rise to inviolable obviation between the wh-phrase and all embedded pronouns that c-command its trace.

Now we have our construction:

(70) At the airport, NP$_0$ met NP$_1$, [who$_k$ ... α_{*k} ... t_k].

As before, two available antecedents NP$_0$ and NP$_1$ represent the truth assignments $x_{i+1} = 0$ and $x_{i+1} = 1$, respectively. The preference function Υ ensures that pronouns in the embedded clause that represent true negative literals of x_{i+1} can only link to the 'false' noun phrase NP$_0$; pronouns that represent true positive literals of x_{i+1} can only link to the 'true' noun phrase NP$_1$. Observe that the relative pronoun who_k may predicate either NP$_0$ or NP$_1$ in the example (70). The strong crossover configuration ensures that an anaphoric element α_{*k} in the extraposed relative clause must obviate the subject of the wh-phrase who_k. Therefore, once the ambiguous predication relation is determined, pronouns representing literals of x_{i+1} must all be linked to the same antecedent because (i) the pronouns must all obviate the predicated noun phrase by strong crossover and (ii) there is only one other permissible antecedent by construction. This exactly corresponds to assigning a consistent truth value to all literals of the Boolean variable x_{i+1}.

The third and final step of the reduction maps each Boolean 3-clause $C_j = (a_j \vee b_j \vee c_j)$ into a pigeonhole gadget. A Boolean clause C_j is true if and only if one of its literals it true. Let us call the literal that satisfies the clause the *selected literal*. Only selected literals need be assigned consistent truth values: nonselected literals simply don't matter, and can receive any arbitrary inconsistent value, or none at all. We have been reducing the quantification of variables to the linking of pronouns, and so must now represent each literal in C_j with a pronoun. For each 3-clause, the reduction builds a sentence that contains three disjoint pronouns and only two possible antecedents. At least one of the pronouns must link to an antecedent outside the sentence — this pronoun represents the selected literal. The following English sentence shows how this works:

(71) [s [the student] thought [the teacher] said that
[he$_a$ introduced him$_b$ to him$_c$]]

Only two preferred antecedents [*the student*] and [*the teacher*] are locally available to the three obviative pronouns he_a, him_b, and him_c in this construction. Therefore at least one of these three pronouns must link to a preferred antecedent available outside the clause, to one of the noun phrases in some dominating quantifier construction — either (63) or (65). This selected pronoun corresponds to a true literal that satisfies the clause C_j under some quantifier-determined truth assignment.

Note that each $\rho(C_j)$ is contained inside $n/2$ VP-ellipsis constructions in the surface representation R. Therefore, according to the copy model the underlying representation corresponding to R will contain $2^{n/2}$ copies of each $\rho(C_j)$, each copy of each $\rho(C_j)$ with its own linking subgraph and its own selected pronoun. This corresponds to the fact that different literals may satisfy a given quantified clause, under different quantifier-determined truth assignments.

Without loss of generality, let a_j be a positive literal of x_i in the 3-clause C_j, and let b_j be a negative literal of x_i in the same 3-clause. Then $\rho(a_j)$ is the pronoun p_{x_i}, and $\rho(b_j)$ is the pronoun $p_{\bar{x}_i}$. The preference function Υ allows each underlying copy of the pronoun p_{x_i} to link to the nonlocally-available antecedent in $\rho(Qx_i)$ that represents the truth assignment $x_i = 1$, and each copy of the pronoun $p_{\bar{x}_i}$ to link to the nonlocally-available antecedent in $\rho(Qx_i)$ that represents the truth assignment $x_i = 0$.

The surface representation R contains $3p$ pronouns (one pronoun for each literal) and $2n + 2p$ available antecedents (two antecedents for each quantifier, and two for each 3-clause). Each pronoun prefers exactly three antecedents: one nonlocal antecedents, and the two local antecedents. For the reduction to be correct, one of the three pronouns in each copy of each $\rho(C_j)$ must link to its single preferred nonlocal antecedent, and the other two pronouns in each copy of $\rho(C_j)$ must link to the two locally available antecedents in that copy of $\rho(C_j)$. No pronoun can be allowed to link to any antecedent that it does not prefer. There are p Boolean 3-clauses, so $p_{\min}$ would be equal to $3p$ if the preference value of a linking were measured in terms of the surface representation. However, the copy model states that linkings are assigned to underlying representations, and so the preference value of a linking must therefore be measured in terms of the underlying representation. For these reasons, $p_{\min}= 3p \cdot 2^{n/2}$, because there are $2^{n/2}$ copies of each pronoun in the underlying representation corresponding to the surface representation R.

In short, there exists a correct referential dependency graph $G = \langle A', O, L \rangle$ with preference value $p_{\min}$ that is also compatible with the underlying representation R' corresponding to R if and only if at least one pronoun in every copy of each $\rho(C_j)$ can link to its sole preferred nonlocal antecedent. This is only possible when each Boolean clause C_j contains at least one true literal for every possible quantifier-determined truth assignment to its literals. Therefore, the surface representation R, preference function Υ and minimum preference value $p_{\min}$ are a positive instance of the Anaphoric Copying Problem if and only if the quantified Boolean formula Ω is true. □

Note that the gadgets used to represent existential quantifiers (65) and Boolean clauses (71) in this proof of lemma 4 can be combined to give a second direct NP-hardness proof for the Anaphoric Preference Problem in the referential dependency model, where each pronoun is no more than four-ways ambiguous and no agreement features or configurations of invisible obviation are used.

The epilogue to this proof is a demonstration of how the preceding reduction might concretely represent the QBF formula (72)

(72) $\forall x_1 \exists x_2 \forall x_3 [(\bar{x}_1 \vee \bar{x}_2 \vee x_3), (x_1 \vee x_2 \vee \bar{x}_3)]$

in the surface representation of an actual English sentence. The surface representation R consists of five components:

- The VP-ellipsis gadget (63) to represent the quantifier $\forall x_1$:

    (73) $[[_{x_1=0}$ some steward$]_1$ [$_{\text{VP}}$ believes that [$_\text{S}$ ...]]$_A$] and so does $[[_{x_1=1}$ some stewardess$]_2$ [$_{\text{VP}}$ e]$_A$]

    We have indicated the overt antecedent of the ellipsed VP by means of the subscript A.

Ellipsis 89

- The strong crossover gadget (70) to represent the quantifier $\exists x_2$:

  (74) $[_S$ at the airport
  $[_{x_2=0}$ a KGB man$]_3$ met $[_{x_2=1}$ the CIA man$]_4$,
  $[_S$ who$_k$ $[\ldots t_k \ldots]]]$

- The VP-ellipsis gadget (63) to represent the quantifier $\forall x_3$:

  (75) $[[_{x_3=0}$ some mechanic$]_5$ $[_{VP}$ suspects that $[_S \ldots]]_B]$
  and so does $[[_{x_3=1}$ some janitor$]_6$ $[_{VP}$ e$]_B]$

  We have indicated the overt antecedent of the ellipsed VP by means of the subscript B.

- The pigeonhole gadget (71) to represent the 3-clause ($\overline{x}_1 \vee \overline{x}_2 \vee x_3$):

  (76) $[_S$ the corporal$_7$ said the sergeant$_8$ hypothesized that $[he_{1,7,8}$ introduced him$_{3,7,8}$ to him$_{6,7,8}]]$

  The subscripts on the pronouns indicate their preferred antecedents. For example, the pronoun $he_{1,7,8}$ prefers the one nonlocal antecedent [*some steward*]$_1$ as well as the two local antecedents *the corporal*$_7$ and *the sergeant*$_8$.

- A second pigeonhole construction to represent the 3-clause ($x_1 \vee x_2 \vee \overline{x}_3$):

  (77) $[_S$ the pilot$_9$ thought the navigator$_{10}$ knew that $[he_{2,9,10}$ traded him$_{4,9,10}$ to him$_{5,9,10}]]$

The resulting surface representation R, in all its glory, is:

(78)
[[$_{x_1=0}$ some steward]$_1$ [$_{VP}$ believes that
[$_S$ at the airport [$_{x_2=0}$ a KGB man]$_3$ met [$_{x_2=1}$ the CIA man]$_4$,
[$_S$ who$_k$
[[$_{x_3=0}$ some mechanic]$_5$ [$_{VP}$ suspects that
[$_S$ the corporal$_7$ said the sergeant$_8$ hypothesized that
[he$_{1,7,8}$ introduced him$_{3,7,8}$ to him$_{6,7,8}$ with t_k]]
and
[$_S$ the pilot$_9$ thought the navigator$_{10}$ knew that
[he$_{2,9,10}$ traded him$_{4,9,10}$ to him$_{5,9,10}$ for t_k]]
]$_B$]
and so does [[$_{x_3=1}$ some janitor]$_6$ [$_{VP}$ e]$_B$]
]]]$_A$]
and so does [[$_{x_1=1}$ some stewardess]$_2$ [$_{VP}$ e]$_A$]

The preference function Υ is as indicated in the subcripts, and the minimum preference value $p_{\min}$ is $2 \cdot 3 \cdot 2^2 = 24$.

As stated, the reduction relies on the extralinguistic information that we modeled with the binary-valued preference function Υ. In the reduction, the preference function ensures that each pronoun links to exactly one of three preferred antecedents, one nonlocal antecedent in a quantifier gadget and two local antecedents in a 3-clause gadget. However, it is possible to replace the preference function in the reduction with a model of linguistic information alone.

The preference function is used by the reduction to enforce two simple constraints. The first constraint is that each pronoun can only link to one nonlocal antecedent in the correct quantifier gadget (in particular, the one nonlocal antecedent that represents the truth assignment that makes the literal that the pronoun represents true). We may accomplish this with agreement features, by making all pronouns that represent positive literals of the same variable agree with each other and with the one nonlocal antecedent that represents the truth assignment that makes the positive literals true. This may be accomplished with one $2n$-valued agreement feature, or with $\log 2n$ binary agreement features, and a paradigm structure where all the pronominal forms are contained in the leaf nodes of the paradigm structure.

The second constraint is that each pronoun in a given 3-clause gadget cannot link to an available antecedent in any of the other 3-clause gadgets. One way to accomplish that is by appeal to the fact that certain local antecedents are prefered to other antecedents solely on the basis of their structural relationship to an anaphoric element in the linguistic representation, such as how proximite the antecedent is to the anaphoric element, whether the antecedent c-commands the anaphoric element, whether the antecedent is a subject or object, and so on. The proposed 3-clause gadget (71) has all these properties. Therefore, the PSPACE lower bound on the complexity of the Anaphora Problem does not crucially depend on the binary-valued preference function Υ or on the extralinguistic information that it models.

This concludes our presentation of lemma 4, in the role of maximizer. In the next section, we assume the role of minimizer.

5.3 Ellipsis Reconsidered

In the preceeding section, the maximizer proved that the Anaphoric Preference Problem is PSPACE-hard in the copy model. Our complexity thesis states that the unitary language computation is NP-complete (see section 1.3.2). Therefore, our thesis predicts that there is a empirical defect in the linguistic analysis that led to the PSPACE-hard copy model of ellipsis. The thesis also tells us exactly where to look for the defect: we must reexamine that part of the linguistic analysis that obligated the language user to perform a computation outside of $\mathcal{NP}$. In the case of a reduction from QBF, the defect must be in that part of the analysis used to support the unnaturally powerful universal quantifier. Therefore, let us reexamine the copy model of ellipsis.

A copy operation naturally predicts that the original and its copy are subject to same post-copying constraints, although operations applied after copying will apply to the original and its copy independently. Neither prediction holds.

The first prediction is that the original (overt) structure and its underlying copy will obey the same post-copying linguistic constraints, including agreement and the binding conditions. If agreement and the binding conditions did not apply after copying, then it would always be possible to vacuously satisfy those constraints, simply by postponing all linking until after copying had applied. Therefore, agreement and the binding conditions must apply both before and after copying.

This expected post-copying equivalence is violated. Although an overt pronoun must agree with its antecedent on person, number, and gender (79a), a copied pronoun can disagree with its antecedents, as in (79b).[3,4]

(79) a. Tom$_1$ read his$_{1/*2}$ book and Barbara$_2$ read his$_{1/*2}$ book (too).
 b. Tom$_1$ [read his$_1$ book] and Barbara$_2$ did [e] too.
  ([read his$_{1/2}$ book])

Moreover, although overt reflexives must have local c-commanding antecedents in (81a), copied reflexives need not, as shown in (81b).[5]

(81) a. [The prisoner$_1$ hung himself$_1$] before [the executioner$_2$ could hang himself$_{*1/2}$].
 b. The prisoner$_1$ [hung himself$_1$] before the executioner$_2$ could [e].
  ([hang himself$_{1/2}$])

The second prediction of the copy model is that operations that apply after copying, such as linking, will apply independently in both the

---

[3] The fact that some English speakers are unable to obtain a covariant interpretation for *Barbara$_1$ read her$_1$ book and Tom did too*, or for *You$_1$ ate your$_1$ vegetables and so did Bob*, does not weaken our criticism of the copy model. Our criticism is based on the necessity of discriminating (79a) and (79b), which the copy model (in its most natural formulation) is unable to do.

[4] Kitagawa [53] proposes to account for this post-copying violation of the agreement condition by postulating a copying rule that deletes the inflectional features of copied anaphoric elements at LF (for some speakers, and as needed to describe their judgements). As Kitagawa himself notes, such a rule predicts the existence of a great many ideolects that are not attested. In particular, the most natural case for Kitagawa's account is where the copying rule simply deletes the gender feature. Then overt *he* can only take masculine singular antecedents and overt *she* can only take feminine singular antecedents, while copied *he* and copied *she* can each take any overt singular antecedent, regardless of gender. The existence of such an ideolect has yet to be confirmed. According to the anaphoric uniqueness condition (AUC) of section 3.3, such an ideolect cannot exist: two pronouns can only behave the same after copying if and only if they behave the same before copying, and so there must always be an asymmetry in the agreement behavior of copied pronouns. We present our account of this (apparent) post-copying agreement clash in section 5.4.

[5] Kitagawa [53] proposes to account for this post-copying violation of binding condition A with a copying rule that turns copied reflexives into pronouns at LF. Such a rule would incorrectly predict that the example (80a) has no possible referential interpretation, because it must violate binding condition B at LF, as shown in (80b). However, for most speakers (80a) has the perfectly natural covariant reading paraphrased in (80c), contra Kitagawa.

(80) a. The prisoner$_1$ [hung himself$_1$] after daring himself$_1$ to [e].
 b. LF: The prisoner$_1$ hung himself$_1$ after daring himself$_1$ to [hang him$_{*1}$].
 c. The prisoner$_1$ [hung himself$_1$] after daring himself$_1$ to *hang himself$_1$*.

Ellipsis   93

original (overt) structure and its underlying copy. This expected post-copying independence is also violated. In particular, linking is not independent in both the original structure and its copy, as shown by example (82), which is incorrectly predicted to have five readings that introduce no new information (two when linking precedes copying, four when linking follows copying, and one overlap).[6]

(82) Bob [introduced Felix to his neighbors] before Max did $[e]$.

In particular, there should be a reading where the overt *his* refers to *Felix* and the ellipsed (copied) *his* refers to *Max*. However, this reading is not available. In fact, only three interpretations of (82) are attested (two invariant, one covariant), as shown in (83).

(83) a. Bob$_1$ [introduced Felix$_2$ to his$_2$ neighbors] and before Max$_3$ did $[e]$.
([*introduce Felix$_2$ to his$_{*1/2/*3}$ neighbors*])
b. Bob$_1$ [introduced Felix$_2$ to his$_1$ neighbors] before Max$_3$ did $[e]$.
([*introduce Felix$_2$ to his$_{1/*2/3}$ neighbors*])

In other words, a pronoun must link to corresponding positions in both the overt verb phrase and its underlying (understood) copy.

This is not real copying, but a kind of higher-order predicate-sharing that can always be represented without copying. We should underlyingly represent a verb phrase as a thematic predicate, that results in a thematic proposition (the sentence) when applied to an argument (the subject of the VP). In VP-ellipsis, the thematic predicate that represents the overt VP is applied to not one but two arguments: the subject of the overt VP and the corresponding subject of the ellipsed VP. The result is still a thematic proposition.

Continuing in this vein, let us represent verbs as higher-order thematic functions that contain a sequence of thematically-typed argument

---

[6] Although Kitagawa's copy theory [53] cannot account for these examples, he does attempt to account for some superficially similar examples as follows. Kitagawa argues that the elliptical utterance *Bob introduced Felix to his neighbors and Max did too* obeys the same "parallelism" constraint that the entirely overt utterance *Bob introduced Felix$_1$ to his neighbors and Max introduced Felix$_1$ to his neighbors too* does. In particular, Kitagawa claims that both utterances incur the same reduction of ambiguity, arguably the effect of the adverb *too*. While our elliptical utterance (82) has only three readings, the corresponding entirely overt utterance *Bob introduced Felix$_1$ to his neighbors before Max introduced Felix$_1$ to his neighbors* has at least seven readings. Therefore, Kitagawa's claim does not rescue the copy theory.

positions. For example, we might represent the English verb *see* as a thematic function $f(2\text{:theme})$, from an argument of type "theme" (the object or entity indirectly involved in the action), to a predicate $f'(1\text{:agent})$ of an argument of type "agent" (the entity initiating the activity). Integers are used to name the argument positions of the thematic function. The subject, direct object, and indirect object of a clause are arguments to the thematic function that represents the main verb of that sentence. Each linguistic argument is assigned a thematic type by the argument position that it saturates in the verb's thematic function.

5.4 Function-Sharing Model of Ellipsis

This line of thinking leads us to the following function-sharing model of ellipsis: (i) the linguistic representation of an utterance includes the thematic structure of the utterance; (ii) an ellipsed VP is an "anaphoric" thematic function whose antecedent is an overt thematic function; (iii) local obviation is a relation between argument positions in a thematic function; and (iv) an anaphoric element may link to an argument or to a local argument position, subject to a suitably extended theory of anaphoric agreement. The function-sharing model also includes the referential dependency model, which maps configurations in the thematic structure into obligatory relations of obviation and immediate antecedence.[7]

This function-sharing model is based on the observation that the overt and null VPs of a VP-ellipsis construction are, in some sense, the same predicate. An anaphoric element inside the shared predicate either refers to a constant, resulting in a invariant interpretation, or it refers to an argument of the predicate, resulting in a covariant interpretation.[8]

Following the proposals above, verbs are represented as higher-order thematic functions from their direct and indirect objects to a predicate, which is itself a thematic function from the subject to a thematic proposition. In a comprehensive thematic representation, the tense of the verb must also be represented a a thematic argument, as the argument that

---

[7] Thematic structure, also called argument structure, is currently an active topic in generative linguistics, with many recent results including [35, 36, 46, 63, 99, 100, 108].

[8] This observation has been made in some form or other, apparently independently, by a wide range of authors [49, 59, 71, 79, 91, 107]. Keenan's work [49] is particularly valuable for the simplicity of its presentation, and Sag's [91] for the breadth of its empirical investigation. Our model incorporates several important refinements to this view, based on the work of Higginbotham [40, 41, 42] and Marantz [66, 67].

saturates the **event** position of the verbal thematic function [40]. The thematic predicate is realized synatactically as a verb phrase, and the thematic proposition is realized as a clause (that is, a sentence). For notational clarity, we will depict the thematic function that represents a given verb by the orthographic form of that verb. For example, we will depict the one-place thematic function that represents the verb *to see* as [see](3:theme), where the '3' names the argument position currently available for saturatation. Unlike the lambda calculus, a thematic function may be freely applied to an argument on its left or on its right.[9]

Then the past tense verb phrase [*saw Jane*] is assigned the thematic structure (84a) and the clause [*Jack saw Jane*] is assigned the thematic structure (84b).

(84)

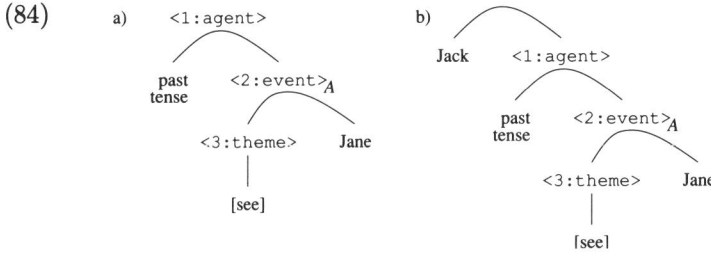

Unfortunately, this notation quickly becomes cumbersome and so for the sake of clarity we will often suppress the **event** argument position. Then the thematic structure assigned to the verb phrase [*saw Jane*] is depicted in (85).

(85) ([saw](2:theme) Jane)(1:agent)

According to the function-sharing model, an ellipsed VP entails an additional application of a pre-existing thematic predicate to an overt

---

[9] We may also wish to characterize the order in which the argument positions of a thematic function are saturated. Although the answer to this question does not impact either our language models or our complexity analysis below, it is nonetheless an interesting question. The answer seems clearest when the thematic function describes an activity or event with a temporal span. Such an event involves a number of roles, such as the initiator or experiencer of the event. Then the earlier in time a given role becomes involved in a given event, the more prominent its argument position is and the later its argument position will be saturated in the thematic function that describes that event [35, 99, 100]. For example, the initiator of an event is inherently the first to be involved in that event, and therefore the agent role is the most prominent role in the thematic function and the last to be discharged. The outcome of such a theory of argument structure is a total order on the argument positions, that holds for all human languages.

argument (the subject of that ellipsed VP). Arguably the simplest way to do this is to represent the ellipsed VP as an "anaphoric" thematic function whose antecedent is an overt thematic function. This is a minor extension to the independently-motivated repertoire of higher-order thematic functions.

For example, the utterance (86a) would be assigned the thematic structure (86b), where the overt VP predicate is applied to both overt subjects.

(86) a. Jack [saw Jane] and Jeff did [e] too.
b.

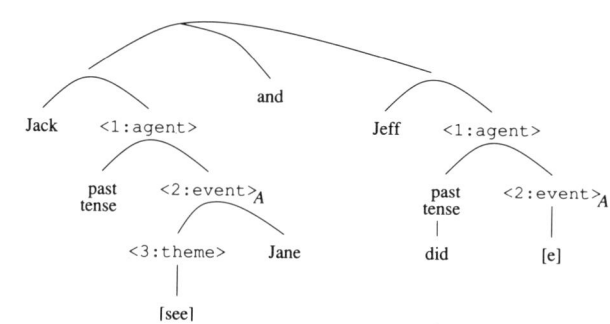

The anaphoric thematic function $\langle 1:\text{agent}\rangle_A$ that applies to the argument *Jeff* is linked to the thematic function [saw Jane]$(1:\text{agent})_A$. In effect, the thematic function of the overt VP (a thematic predicate) is being applied "in parallel" to two independent arguments.

The thematic structure may contain series of links, from a chain of anaphoric thematic functions to an overt thematic function, which will give the appearance of "recursive" ellipsis, as in (52) in section 5.1 above.

In order to account for the facts of invisible obviation, we shall require local obviation to be a relation between the argument positions in the VP predicate, as illustrated in (87b) for the utterance (87a).

(87) a. Jesse [likes him] and Mark does [e] too.
    b.
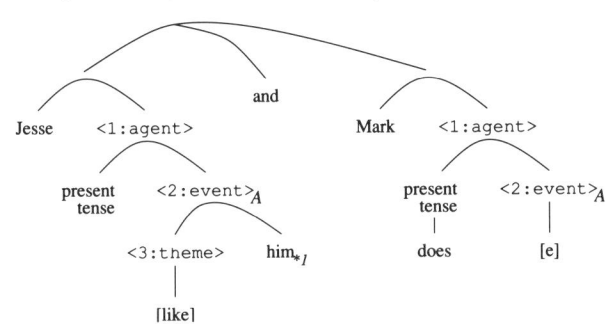

That is, argument positions 3 and 1 are mutually obviative in the thematic function for the verb *like*, according to the binding condition B. Therefore, when the pronoun *him* saturates position 3, it in turn obviates whatever argument saturates position 1. In the VP-ellipsis configuration (87), the corresponding subjects *Jesse* and *Mark* saturate argument position 1 of the shared VP predicate and so *him* must obviate both subjects, a fact that was described in section 4.1.4 by the invisible obviation condition (IOC). The thematic structure representation relevant to the function-sharing model straightforwardly explains the IOC, without the unnaturally powerful copying operation of the copy model.

The reader will note that the difficulty of depicting link and obviate relations has forced us to use subscripts here. In particular, $\text{link}(\alpha, \beta)$ is depicted by assigning α and β the same subscript, while $\text{obviate}(\alpha, \beta)$ is depicted by assigning α the subscript assigned to β preceeded by an asterisk '*'. Referential dependencies between thematic functions will be depicted by upper-case alphabetic subscripts (A), wherease those between arguments will bbe depicted by lower-case alphabetic subscripts (i) and those between argument positions will be depicted by integer subscripts (1).

In order to account for the facts of invariant and covariant interpretations of anaphoric elements in VP-ellipsis, we allow an anaphoric element to link to a linguistic element directly, resulting in the invariant interpretation, or indirectly, to an argument position in the thematic function, resulting in the covariant interpretation. This is depicted in (88b), where the pronoun *his* may link to *Felix* directly, which we depict by assigning the subscript i to his_i and $Felix_i$, or indirectly, to argument postion 1, which we depict by assigning the subscript 1 to his_1.

(88) a. Felix [hates his neighbors] and so does Max [e].
  b.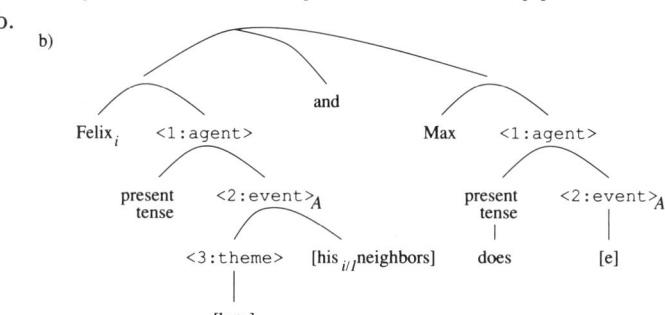

The fact that certain anaphoric elements (such as reflexives and reciprocals) and certain antecedents (such as quantified noun phrases) require a covariant interpretation may be easily described in the function-sharing model. First, reflexives and reciprocals can only link to argument positions. Second, an anaphoric element α cannot link directly to a quantified noun phrase β that c-commands α; rather, α must link to the argument position that is saturated by β.

The Anaphoric Uniqueness Condition (AUC) constrains an antecedence relation between two arguments a linguistic representation. Therefore, it not clear how the AUC should constrain this new relation between an argument and an argument position — for example, what does it means for an anaphoric element to subsume an argument position? Therefore, we must also extend the AUC to the case where an anaphoric element links to an argument position in a thematic function.

Given that we have extended the range of link to include argument positions, we must rephrase the AUC to state that an anaphoric element α may link to an argument position i if and only if α agrees with the overt argument β that saturates i. As before, an anaphoric element α may be linked to an argument β directly if and only if α is the most specific anaphoric element that subsumes β in the paradigm structure.

Recall the curious agreement asymmetry that arises in the covariant interpretation of anaphoric elements, as illustrated in (89).

(89) a. Tom_1 [read his_1 book] and $Barbara_2$ did [e] too.
      ([read $his_{1/2}$ book])
  b. $Barbara_2$ [read her_2 book] and Tom_1 did [e] too.
      ([read $her_{*1/2}$ book])

The covariant interpretation of *her* is not possible in (89b), apparently due to an agreement clash between *her* and *Tom*. However, the covariant interpretation of *his* is possible in (89a), despite the apparent agreement clash between *his* and *Barbara*.

We were motivated to postulate an asymmetry between the English pronouns *he* and *she* in section 3.3 above. There we argued that *he* was the pure third person singular pronoun, that therefore dominates the third person singular feminine pronoun *she* in the paradigm structure for English pronouns, as depicted in figure 3.2. Let us suppose that the inflectional features of an anaphoric element α are incorporated into the selectional restrictions of an argument position i when α links to i. Then α's inflectional features must subsume the inflectional features of every argument that saturates the position i. The net effect is that the inflectional features of an ellipsed anaphoric element must subsume those of its overt antecedent in the covariant interpretation. This accounts for the agreement asymmetry illustrated in (89) in an entirely natural manner.

Our function-sharing model also correctly predicts that the example (82), repeated here as (90a), has only the one thematic structure shown in (90b).

(90) a. Bob [introduced Felix to his neighbors] before Max did [e]
    b.
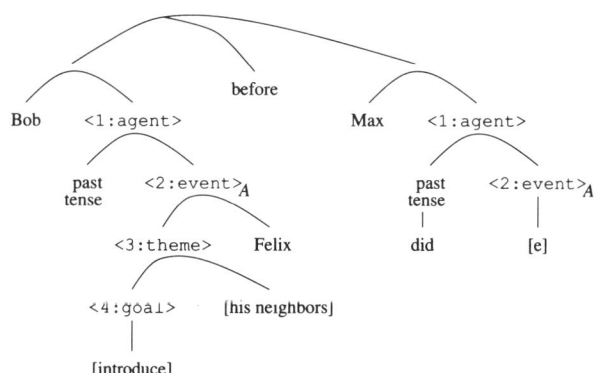

The thematic structure (90b) contains one anaphoric element (*his*) that may potentially link to any of the three available antecedents (*Bob*, *Felix*, and *Max*) or to any of three argument positions in the [introduce] thematic function. In fact, there are exactly five correct referential dependency graphs compatible with (90b), as shown in (91,92).

The pronoun *his* can freely link to each of the three available antecedents, as shown in (91), although the reading where his_k links to Max_k is not particularly salient.

(91)
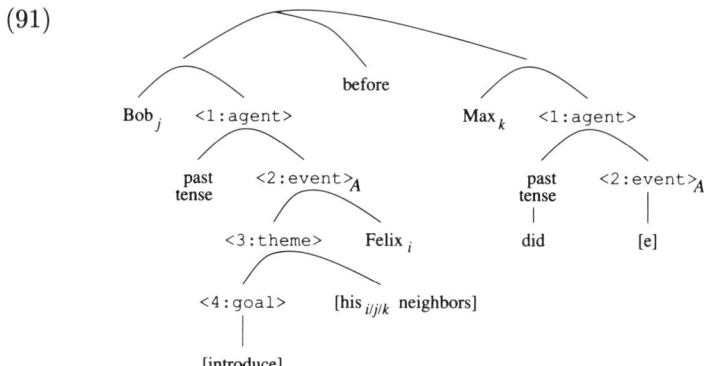

The pronoun *his* may also link to argument positions 1 and 2 in the introduce thematic function, as shown in (92). The pronoun *his* cannot link to position 3 without creating a circular referential dependency, because it is contained inside a phrase that saturates position 3.

(92)
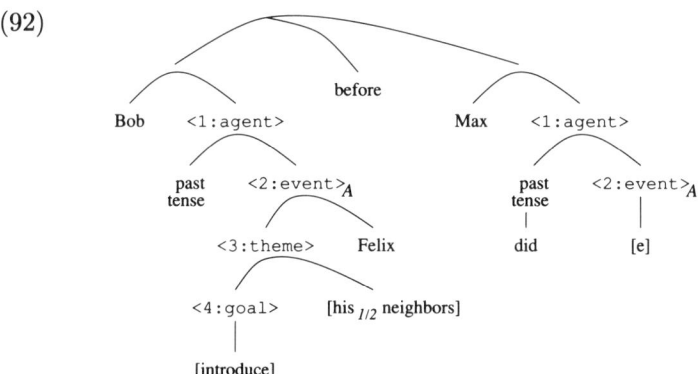

The interpretation where his_2 links to argument postion 2 is indistinguishable from the interpetation in (91) where his_i links to the argument $Felix_i$, and so our function-sharing model correctly predicts that the anaphoric element in the utterance (90a) has four distinct interpretations, of which three are salient. The two salient invariant intepretations are represented in (91) as $him_{i/j}$ and the one salient covariant interpretation is represented in (92) as him_1.

The function-sharing model is conceptually simple. Moreover, it is superior to the copy model on empirical grounds alone because it more accurately represents the language user's knowledge of ellipsed anaphoric elements. A more detailed empirical investigation of syntactic ellipsis, whose outcome supports the function-sharing model, may be found in [85, appendix B].

To recap, the function-sharing model of ellipsis states that (i) the linguistic representation of an utterance includes the thematic structure of the utterance; (ii) an ellipsed VP is an "anaphoric" thematic function whose antecedent is an overt thematic function; (iii) local obviation is a relation between argument positions in a thematic function; (iv) an anaphoric element may link to any argument (other than a QNP) or to a local argument position, subject to the extended anaphoric uniqueness condition; (v) reflexives and reciprocals must link to local argument positions. The function-sharing model also includes the referential dependency model, which maps configurations in the thematic structure into obligatory relations of obviation and immediate antecedence.

Let us conclude our presentation by specializing the Anaphoric Preference Problem to the function-sharing model. Recall that the Anaphoric Preference Problem is the problem of computing the maximally-preferred correct referential dependency graph G compatible with a given linguistic representation R that lacks only relations of referential dependency. The central difference between the copy model and the function-sharing model is how the referential dependency graph is constructed. In the copy model, the RDG is constructed both before and after all ellipsed material has been explicitly "reconstructed" by a recursive copy operation. In the function-sharing model, the RDG is constructed directly from the thematic structure, which is a transparent representation of the linguistic properties of the overt elements in an utterance.

The only motivation for the underlying representation of the copy model was to represent the language user's knowledge of anaphora in conjunction with syntactic ellipsis. Fortunately, the thematic structure referred to by the function-sharing model is not so narrowly motivated. Thematic functions are independently needed to represent the language user's knowledge of utterances, even those without anaphoric elements or ellipsed material. The function-sharing model simply extends the thematic function representation to account for facts about the language user's interpretation of ellipsed anaphoric elements, such as invisible obviation and covariant and invariant interpretations. Its extensions are relatively minor: to allow anaphoric thematic functions to link to overt thematic functions, to allow local argument positions to obviate each other, and to allow anaphoric elements to link to argument positions as well as to arguments themselves.

For these reasons, we define the Anaphoric Preference Problem in this function-sharing model ("Anaphoric Sharing") as follows. The input consists of a paradigm structure P for anaphoric elements, a preference function Υ, and a complete thematic structure R lacking only relations of referential dependency among arguments and argument positions. R contains thematic functions with the saturated argument positions I as well as the 3-tuple $\langle A^A, A^B, A^C \rangle$ of disjoint sets of arguments A, and R explicitly represents all anaphoric thematic functions and their antecedent functions. The output is a correct referential dependency graph $G = \langle A, I, O, L \rangle$ with the maximally-preferred linking L that is compatible with the thematic structure R, where $L \subset (A^A \cup A^B) \times (A \cup I)$ and $O \subseteq (A \times A) \cup (I \times I)$. The corresponding decision problem is to decide whether or not there exists a correct RDG G with preference value at least $p_{\min}$ that is compatible with the thematic structure R.

Let us now analyze the computational complexity of this Anaphoric Sharing Problem.

5.5 An $\mathcal{NP}$ Algorithm for Anaphoric Sharing

The reduction used to prove lemma 4 is not possible with the function-sharing model of ellipsis. Even better for the minimizer, we can prove that the Anaphora Problem is in NP according to the comprehensive language model that is the outcome of the language complexity game played to date.

LEMMA 5 *Anaphoric Sharing is in $\mathcal{NP}$.*

Proof 6 We outline a simple nondeterministic polynomial time algorithm that solves the Anaphoric Sharing Problem. The input to our algorithm consists of a preference function Υ, minimal preference value $p_{\min}$, and a complete thematic structure R that contains thematic functions with the saturated argument positions I as well as the 3-tuple

$\langle A^A, A^B, A^C \rangle$ of disjoint sets of arguments. R explicitly represents all anaphoric thematic functions and their antecedent functions. On such an input, our algorithm outputs a correct referential dependency graph $G = \langle A, I, O, L \rangle$ with a linking L whose preference value at least $p_{\min}$ that is compatible with the thematic structure R, if and only if such an RDG exists. The linking relation L includes links from the anaphoric elements $A^A \cup A^B$ to the arguments A and to the argument positions I. The obviation relation O includes obviation between pairs of arguments in A, as well as between argument positions in the same thematic function.

Our algorithm consists of four stages. In the first and second stages, we deterministically map configurations in R into the corresponding set O of obligatory obviate relations, and a set $\mathcal{L}$ of all the possible link relations compatible with R. In the third stage, we nondeterministically guess a potentially correct subset L of $\mathcal{L}$ such that every anaphoric element is linked to exactly one antecedent in L. In the fourth (final) stage, we deterministically verify that the preference value of L is at least $p_{\min}$, and that the resulting RDG $G = \langle A, I, O, L \rangle$ is in fact correct (that is, it satisfies the Extended AUC and preserves the semantics of obviation).

The first stage maps configurations in R into the obligatory obviation relations O, $O \subseteq (A \times A) \cup (I \times I)$. If an argument β locally c-commands an overt argument α in R, $\alpha \in A^B \cup A^C$, then the argument positions assigned to α and β are obviative in O. If an argument γ nonlocally c-commands an overt referring expression β, $\beta \in A^C$, then γ and β are obviative in O. If an anaphoric element α c-commands the trace t_k of a wh-phrase ω_k that c-commands α, then α obviates the subject predicated by ω. The resulting obviation relation O is exactly the obviation relation compatible with the representation R.

The arguments A are in a many-to-one correspondence with a subset of the argument positions I. If two arguments are obviative in O, then the argument positions that they saturate cannot also be obviative in O. Therefore, in the absolute worst case, all arguments are mutually obviative and so $|O| \leq |A|^2$. The question of whether a given pair of arguments (or the argument positions that they saturate) are obviative can be decided in time proportional to the number of wh-phrases in R according to the referential dependence model, and so this first stage requires determinisitic time $O(|R| \cdot |A|^2)$.

The second stage maps configurations in R into the maximal linking $\mathcal{L}$ compatible with R, $\mathcal{L} \subset (A^A \cup A^B) \times (A \cup I)$. If an argument position i is saturated by an argument β that locally c-commands a reflexive or reciprocal α in R, then $\mathsf{link}(\alpha, i)$ is included in $\mathcal{L}$. If a silent PRO α in A^B is controlled by an argument β, then $\mathsf{link}(\alpha, \beta)$ is included in $\mathcal{L}$. If an overt pronoun α in A^B does not obviate an argument β that saturates position i, then $\mathsf{link}(\alpha, \beta)$ and $\mathsf{link}(\alpha, i)$ are included in $\mathcal{L}$. Finally, all links to quantified noun phrases are removed from $\mathcal{L}$, as are all links that violate the Extended AUC. The resulting link relation $\mathcal{L}$ contains every correct link relation compatible with R.

In the worst case $\mathcal{L}$ contains links from every anaphoric element in $A^A \cup A^B$ to every argument in A and every argument position saturated by an argument in A, and so $|\mathcal{L}| < |A^A \cup A^B| \cdot 2|A|$. The question of whether a given anaphoric element may link to a given argument or argument position can be decided in constant time according to the referential dependence model, and so this second stage requires deterministic time $O(|A|^2)$.

The third stage nondeterministically guesses a correct subset L of $\mathcal{L}$ where each anaphoric element is linked to exactly one argument or argument position. If any anaphoric element in $A^A \cup A^B$ is not linked to some argument or argument position in L in a manner that satisfies the Extended AUC, or if the minimal preference value $p_{\min}$ exceeds the preference value $\Upsilon(L)$ of the guessed linking L, then the algorithm rejects its guess. The resulting linking L is a forest of trees, where each available antecedent in A^C is the root of its own tree, and each anaphoric element in $A^A \cup A^B$ is an interior or leaf vertex of a tree whose unique root vertex is an available antecedent. This stage requires nondeterministic time proportional to the number of links in $\mathcal{L}$, or time $O(|A|^2)$.

The fourth stage verifies that the guessed linking L is in fact correct (that is, obeys the semantics of obviation relations). Let L_i be the linking relation induced from L, with each link from an anaphoric element α to an argument position i replaced by all induced links from α to arguments that saturate position i:

$$L_i \doteq \{(\alpha, \beta) \ : \ \exists \alpha \in (A^A \cup A^B), \exists \beta \in A \\ [(\alpha, \beta) \in L \ \vee \ \exists i \in I[(\alpha, i) \in L \ \wedge \ \mathsf{saturate}(\beta, i)]]\}$$

Although each argument in A must saturate exactly one argument position in R, each argument position may be saturated by more than one argument (for example, in ellipsis). An anaphoric element α linked to exactly one argument position in L may be linked to more than one argument in L_i, which will give rise to a covariant interpretation. Each argument in A has at most one "outgoing" edge in L, each argument saturates at most one argument position in R, and so L_i has no more than $2 \cdot |A|$ edges.

For each anaphoric element α, $\alpha \in A^A \cup A^B$, we compute the set $D(\alpha)$ of all available antecedents that α depends on, that is:

$$D(\alpha) \doteq \{\gamma : \gamma \in A^C \wedge (\alpha, \gamma) \in L_i^+\}$$

Let $D = \{D(\alpha) : \alpha \in A^A \cup A^B\}$. D may be computed by depth-first search on the transpose of L_i (L_i^T), starting from the "root" vertices A^C, in time proportional to the number of anaphoric elements times the number of available antecedents, that is, in deterministic time $O(|A|^2)$.

Similarly, let O_i be the obviation relation induced from O, with each obviation relation between a pair (i, j) of argument positions replaced by all induced obviation relations between arguments that saturate those argument positions:

$$\begin{aligned} O_i \doteq \{(\alpha, \beta) \quad : \quad & \exists \alpha \in A, \; \exists \beta \in A \\ & [(\alpha, \beta) \in O \; \vee \; \exists i, j \in I \\ & [(i, j) \in O \wedge \mathsf{saturate}(\alpha, i) \wedge \mathsf{saturate}(\beta, j)]]\} \end{aligned}$$

The induced obviation relation O_i may be computed in deterministic time $O(|A|^2)$.

Finally, for each $\mathsf{obviate}(\alpha, \beta) \in O_i$, our algorithm rejects the guess L if $\exists \gamma \in A^C$ such that $\gamma \in D(\alpha)$ and $\gamma \in D(\beta)$.[10] There are at most $|A|^2$ obviation edges in O_i, each of which may be verified in time proportional to the number of available antecedents A^C, and so the final stage may be performed in deterministic time $O(|A|^3)$.

The algorithm accepts its input if and only if it is possible to compute an obviation relation O from R and then guess a linking L with preference value at least $p_{\min}$ such that L satisfies the Extended AUC and

---

[10] Although our function-sharing model does not exclude circular dependencies [39], we may efficiently check that the linking L does not involve any circular dependencies, by first computing the positive transitive closure of the dependency relation:

$\mathsf{depend}(\alpha, \beta) \doteq \exists \gamma [(\alpha, \gamma) \in L_i \wedge (\gamma, \beta) \in \mathsf{dom}^+]$

Then our algorithm rejects if any anaphoric element depends on itself, that is, if $\exists \alpha$ such that $\mathsf{depend}^+(\alpha, \alpha)$.

the resulting referential dependency graph $G = \langle A, I, O, L \rangle$ is correct and compatible with the input thematic representation R. The entire algorithm runs in nondeterministic time $O(|R|^3)$. □

As can be seen from section 5.3, the function-sharing model assigns more accurate linguistic representations to the class of elliptical utterances than the copy model does, and no utterances are assigned more accurate representations by the copy model. However, the significance of the function-sharing model goes beyond merely the number of additional linguistic examples correctly represented.

Recall that our central scientific goal is to understand the comprehension, production, and acquisition of human language. Modern generative linguistic theory is interesting only in so far as it advances this goal. The output of a PSPACE-hard computation may be exponentially large in the size of the corresponding input. (Unlike problems in $\mathcal{NP}$, PSPACE-hard problems are not thought to have efficient witnesses. Recall that an efficient witness is a short correctness proof for a solution. In the case of the Anaphora Problem, a correct graph of referential dependencies serves as the correctness proof.) If the Anaphoric Preference Problem were PSPACE-hard, as it is according to the copy model of ellipsis, then the mental representations required to produce and comprehend ellipsed anaphora would likely be infeasibly large. Certain utterances containing ellipsed anaphora could not be feasibly represented, and therefore language users could neither comprehend nor produce such utterances. Therefore, current linguistic theories of ellipsis and covariant interpetations would not be falsifiable, nor would they yield a plausible account of language comprehension and production.

So, by reducing the complexity of the Anaphora Problem from at least PSPACE to at most $\mathcal{NP}$, we demonstrate that the Anaphora Problem does have efficient witnesses, and in turn show that current generative linguistic theory does in fact form the basis of a plausible account of language computations involving anaphora and ellipsis.

We may combine our results to obtain the following theorem.

THEOREM 2 The Anaphoric Sharing Problem is NP-complete.

Proof 7 Anaphoric Sharing, the Anaphoric Preference Problem in the function-sharing model, is in NP by lemma 5. It is NP-hard by the NP-hardness of the Anaphora Problem in the referential dependence model (theorem 1), the fact that the function-sharing model includes the complete referential dependence model, and the fact that the Anaphora Problem is a proper subproblem of the Anaphoric Preference Problem (by definition). □

As an epiloque to this tight upper and lower bound on the complexity of the Anaphoric Sharing Problem, let us briefly speculate how we may plausibly upper bound the complexity of the broad Anaphora Problem in the "true" empirically correct language model.

First, we may conjecture that the number of covert elements in a linguistic representation is directly proportional to the number overt elements in the linguistic representation. The reason is, in order for a covert element to participate in a linguistic representation, it must be related to an overt element by means of a fixed number of known linguistic relations, such as immediate antecedence, obviation, domination, or saturation. Therefore, the total number of elements in a linguistic representation should be roughly proportional to the number of overt elements in that representation.

In particular, covert arguments in a linguistic representation are either coreferential with an overt argument in the representation (as in the case of controlled PRO or wh-trace), in which case their corresponding vertices in the graph of referential dependencies may in effect be coalesced, or they are assigned an arbitrary interpretation (in the case of PRO_{arb}), in which case they do not participate in the graph of referential dependencies and may be ignored entirely. Other aspects of a linguistic representation, such as the representation of quantifier scope, do not increase the number of arguments. Therefore, the number of obviation relations in a linguistic representation should be at most quadratic in the number of overt arguments, an upper bound that is obtained in the case of a complete obviation graph.

We have also seen that the correspondence between a referential dependency graph G and the complete linguistic representation R to which it belongs has a simple structure. In every case we have examined, simple configurations in the representation R are mapped into specified portions of the graph G in a straightforward, easily computed manner. Therefore, we may reasonably conjecture that the broad Anaphora Problem is also in $\mathcal{NP}$, and therefore NP-complete as well.

To summarize, in the previous chapter 4 we proved that the Anaphora Problem was NP-hard in the referential dependence model. In this chapter, we argued that including the computationally complex phenomenon of syntactic ellipsis in our language model for anaphora does not increase the complexity of the Anaphora Problem outside of $\mathcal{NP}$. Let us therefore suspend the language complexity game for anaphora in this quiescent state, and consider its implications for the study of human language.

6 Implications of the Results

This chapter reviews the implications of our three central results for the study of human language. We consider how each result advances our understanding of language, and what it implies for current approaches to the study of language, including generative linguistics, computational linguistics, and psycholinguistics. Recall our three results: a coherent interpretation of human language; a complexity thesis for human language; and several rounds of the language complexity game, resulting in a precise, empirically-motivated description of language computations related to anaphora.

In section 6.1, we first explain how our interpretation of human language resolves three conceptual puzzles inherent in the framework of generative linguistics, and hence is preferred on conceptual grounds. Then we argue that the machine parsing of linguistic expressions cannot achieve a useful level of performance because it inaccurately models the process of human language comprehension. In section 6.2, we examine the implications of our complexity thesis for theories of language processing (performance) and linguistic knowledge (competence). In section 6.3, we broadly compare our research method (the language complexity game) and its technical results to the methods of generative linguistics and the technical results obtained in that conceptual framework.

6.1 Interpretation of Human Language

We have modeled human language as a unitary computation whose input is extralinguistic information i and a language hypothesis M, and whose output is a revised language hypothesis M' and a representation of the linguistic information in i according to M. Extralinguistic information is the output of other cognitive models, including sensations, intentions, beliefs, models of agents, the mental lexicon, the conceptual system, and so forth. A particular human language M is the set of all linguistic representations possible in that language, including partial representations. The universal grammar $\mathcal{M}$ is the set of all possible human languages, that defines the domain and range of the unitary language computation $f(i, M) = \langle r, M' \rangle$.

Let us compare the conceptual framework of our investigation to other conceptual frameworks for the study of human language. Our discussion encompasses generative linguistics, the competence/performance distinction [15], computational linguistics and natural language processing, and Marr's levels of computational abstraction [69]. In section 6.1.1, we discuss three conceptual difficulties inherent in these other conceptual frameworks and explain how they are resolved under our proposed interpretation of language. Next, in section 6.1.2 we define the Parsing Problem to be the problem of assigning structural descriptions to the symbolic expressions of a formal language according to a formal grammar of that language's syntax. We argue that this Parsing Problem is an incorrect, ill-posed statement of the language comprehension problem and therefore machine parsing is unlikely to match human linguistic performance.

Let us now consider the implications of our proposed interpretation of human language for the scientific study of language.

6.1.1 The Study of Language

A conceptual framework within which to study human language must answer three questions:

1. What is language?
2. What is a theory of language?
3. How can the research problem of understanding language be divided up so that the solutions to subproblems may ultimately be combined?

Generative linguistics holds that:

1. Language is an innate cognitive system of knowledge;
2. A theory of language is an explicit procedure for enumerating the set of complete, well-formed representations of that linguistic knowledge; and
3. We postulate subclasses of linguistic representations to explain aspects of linguistic knowledge, intending ultimately to combine these postulated representations.

Three conceptual puzzles arise in the study of language, and remain unresolved in the generative framework.

The first puzzle is how language can be both complex and yet easy to use. Linguistics tells us that language is a complex system. Computer science tells us that complex systems do not perform efficiently. Yet language processing seems effortlessly efficient. How can this be? This is Cordemoy's paradox, named after the Cartesian linguist Géraud de Cordemoy who observed, "We can scarce believe, seeing the facility there is in speaking, that there should need so many parts to be acted for that purpose: But we must accustom ourselves by admiring the structure of our Body, to consider that 'tis made by an incomparable workman, who is inimitable."[25, pp.84–5] Cordemoy's paradox is reduced to near contradiction in the framework of generative linguistics, where the problem of using linguistic knowledge is certainly intractable.

The second puzzle is why the language of comprehension ($\mathcal{L}_c$) is equivalent to the language of production ($\mathcal{L}_p$). (The language of comprehension is what the language user is able to comprehend; the language of production is what the language user is able to produce.) A priori, the processes of comprehension and production seem independent. The computational problems encountered in the comprehension and production of utterances are vastly different. So much so, that the coupled devices of engineered communication systems (such as encoder/decoder or transmitter/receiver pairs) employ different algorithms, different representations, and even different machine architectures. Successful communication in these engineered systems is possible only because of designer intent. In the absence of an attentive God that designed our language ability for the purposes of communication, this fact would lead us to expect a human race where $\mathcal{L}_c$ and $\mathcal{L}_p$ did not always overlap, contrary to observed fact. (Or imagine a new-made race of people, where males can understand the utterances of females but not of other males, and females can understand the utterances of males but not of other females. Not only is this scenerio as likely *a priori* as one where the languages of comprehension and production are equivalent, but it enjoys a significant selective advantage: males and females would immediately pair up, in order to reap the purported survival benefits of linguistic communication.)

Comprehension and production must inherently share something, but what? According to generative linguistics, $\mathcal{L}_c$ and $\mathcal{L}_p$ are equivalent because they involve the same linguistic knowledge. But how is this knowledge (a finite generative procedure) used in the comprehension and production of utterances? No satisfactory answer to this question is currently known, nor can one plausibly be considered forthcoming.

Lacking an answer to this question, we have failed to answer the original question, namely, why $\mathcal{L}_c = \mathcal{L}_p$?

The third puzzle is how to characterize language comprehension independent of the producer's intentions. It would seem that "successful comprehension" must be defined as "comprehending what the producer intended." Yet the producer's intention is not available to the comprehender as an input. So how then can we adequately characterize the process of language comprehension? Comprehension cannot mean to find *some* structural description of the utterance, because this allows the null structural description as a trivial (non)solution. Nor can it mean to find *all* possible structural descriptions for the utterance, because this does not tell us which one is the "intended" structural description. The current linguistic frameworks do not resolve this puzzle.

These foundational puzzles are best resolved by the conceptual framework within which particular theories are to be proposed. A conceptual framework does not itself answer empirical questions. Rather, it explains how these questions will be answered by particular theories.

The conceptual framework of our investigation may be summarized as follows:

1. Language is a unitary computation from the forms produced by other cognitive systems — including the mental lexicon, models of speaker's intentions and listener's state, and motor, sensory, and conceptual systems — to the linguistic representation that best describes those forms (that is, the representation that most reduces the apparent information in those forms);
2. A theory of language is an explicit characterization of the unitary language computation, at an empirically-justified level of computational abstraction;
3. For each natural subclass of linguistic representations, we describe a computation that outputs those linguistic representations, given the necessary information as input. The necessary information may include other subclasses of linguistic representations, as well as the outputs of other cognitive systems.

An overt linguistic expression, a kind of idealized language percept, constitutes only a very small part of the total instantaneous information available to the language faculty. The more information available to the language faculty, the more complete the linguistic representation of that information will be, and the less random the information appears to the language faculty.

The goal of this monograph, then, is to describe the mental computations performed by language users. The computations described in this monograph are all attributed to language users. Our descriptions are framed in terms of abstract problem statements, because there is insufficient empirical evidence to justify a more detailed description of these mental computations. A computational problem specifies the mapping from inputs to outputs abstractly, without describing how that mapping is to be performed by a finite computing machine. Given our current understanding, a theory of language computations couched in terms of algorithms or state transition sequences alone (without first specifying the computational problem to be solved) cannot possibly be scientifically valid.

In contrast, generative linguistics uses computation as a tool, to explicitly describe the infinite space of linguistic representations. The computations found in generative linguistics are *not* attributed to the language user. The computations of generative linguistics are framed in terms of explicit algorithms (such as grammars) and sequences of discrete state transitions (such as derivations), because a more abstract description in terms of problem statements would not be constructive. A generative linguistic theory couched in terms of computational problems alone (without providing algorithms to solve those problems) would not be sufficiently constructive.

Our proposed interpretation of what language is explains how the preceding puzzles are to be resolved.

A linguistic representation is the best representation of the available extralinguistic information. The best representation of partial or incomplete information is an incomplete representation. Therefore, language computations need never perform a blind search that can lead to computational intractability. Human language does not assign a complete representation to computationally-inaccessible information, even though some complete representation might be consistent with the information. By "incomplete information" we mean that the computationally-accessible information in the input does not suffice to uniquely determine a complete linguistic representation. This is the perspective of computational information theory [112], rather than the classical information theory [94], because we do not provide an unbounded amount of computational resources with which to process the input information.

Our proposed framework suggests an answer to Cordemoy's paradox, namely, that language is the process of efficiently constructing the best representation of *all* the extralinguistic information. On our view, the language faculty is not informationally encapsulated. As is well-known, an informationally-encapsulated system is inherently inefficient, both computationally and statistically. Restricting the amount of information available to a computational module results in a computational inefficiency because that module is unable to prune nondeterministic branches in its computation tree as early as it might otherwise be able to. It results in a statistical inefficiency because a module might need to examine all available information in order to determine the optimal estimate, cf. [105]. In short, the only modules in human language are abstract *knowledge* modules, not computational modules of any kind.

On this view, language cannot be the computational module that Fodor [29] argues it is, because language computations are not informationally encapsulated. Contra Fodor, this is desirable because it is the only way to explain why language comprehension is possible at all in the face of wild sensory underdetermination. If the only input to language comprehension were a sensation, or even an abstract uncorrupted symbolic expression, then the problem of constructing anything like the intended representation would be ill-posed in a serious way. The same is true for a statement of the language production problem whose sole input was a representation of meaning.

According to our proposed interpretation, language production and language comprehension are fundamentally the same process, from cognitive forms to linguistic representations. They differ only in that language production is typically correlated motor activity, while language comprehension typically is not. The fact that language production is characteristically associated with movement of the producer's vocal tract does not imply that this vocal tract motion is the output of language production. The output of language production is a linguistic representation, which includes instructions to the sensori-motor system that may or may not be executed according to the conscious volition of the language user. Motor instructions may be executed equally well during language comprehension as in language production. Our framework therefore achieves true Cartesian separation between the process of constructing mental representations, and the perceptual information that justifies a particular mental representation. Note, however, that our proposed framework fails to provide any understanding of the creative aspects of production that so concerned Cartesians.

Our proposed interpretation defines comprehension without reference to the producer's intentions, because comprehension and production always compute the best representation of the available information. When the extralinguistic information available to the comprehender (from the cognitive model of the speaker's intentions, the sensory system, and the priming of lexical entries, for example) is roughly equivalent to the extralinguistic information available to the producer, then the comprehender constructs the same representation that the producer intended.

The proposed conceptual framework also suggests a way to understand the relationship between generative linguistic theory and a computational model of the language user. A generative grammar is a constructive theory of the informational dependencies in the extra-linguistic mental codes. As such, it enumerates the set of complete structural descriptions, and thereby provides a partial, extensional characterization of the relation between extra-linguistic codes and their structural descriptions: extensional because a generative grammar only describes the set of possible outputs, and partial because this set is limited to complete structural descriptions of complete, uncorrupted expressions. For these reasons, a generative theory is arguably a necessary first step in the design of an adequate theory of human language.

However, the generative theory does *not* specify the function to be computed by the language model. For one, the input to the two computations is not the same. The input to the unitary language computation is the set of codes produced by the other cognitive systems (that is, the extralinguistic information); the input to a generative grammar is an underlying form, which is the index of enumeration. Nor are the possible outputs of the two computations the same. The unitary language computation assigns a structural description to every input, and therefore the set of possible outputs must include partial representations, for incomplete extralinguistic information. In contrast, a generative grammar only enumerates complete structural descriptions (cf. [47]). Generative grammar and unitary language computation also specify different relations between a structural description and the symbolic expression that is its overt terminal string yield. The generative grammar specifies a relation between complete structural descriptions and complete, noise-free symbolic expressions. The language computation specifies a relation between structural descriptions and extralinguistic information; the relation between structural descriptions and their overt expressions is an almost inconsequential subset of this relation, that also includes structural descriptions for incomplete or noisy expressions. For these reasons, a parser cannot be a model of human language, or even plausibly part of such a model.[1]

This is simply to say, generative theory is not a model of human language, at any level of abstraction. Rather, it is a model of linguistic knowledge. These points are subtle, and have confused many prominent researchers. No less a scientist than Marr [69] has confused the distinction between competence and performance with levels of computational abstraction. But, as we have seen, the relationship between competence and performance is not one of abstraction. Competence and performance are simply entirely different classes of computations, both of which may be described at different levels of abstraction. (For alternate interpretations of the relation between generative grammar and human language, at odds with the one presented here, see, for example, [8, 9, 15, 17, 89, 97].)

Generative linguistic theory has therefore been obligated to distinguish knowledge of language (competence) and the use of that knowledge (performance).[2] An ability "can improve or decline, can be inadequate to determine consequences of knowledge, and so on. [Knowledge], however, remains stable while our ability to use it changes, and we have

---

[1]A language model is a function from the changing extralinguistic information, which looks nothing like an abstract string of terminal symbols, to the best structural description of that information. A parser is a function from a string of terminal symbols to that set of structural descriptions whose yield exhausts that symbol-string. Hence it is reasonable to maintain, in the words of Berwick and Weinberg, that "the theory of grammar....specifies the function to be computed by the parser." [8, p.82] However true that statement is, parsing is at best weakly related to the comprehension, production, and acquisition of human languages.

[2]The distinction between competence and performance has historically been intertwined with a prescriptive theory of linguistic normalcy, with a distinction between language and cognition, and with an idealization to a homogeneous language community: "Linguistic theory is concerned primarily with an ideal speaker-listener, in a completely homogeneous speech-community, who knows its language perfectly and is unaffected by such grammatically irrelevant conditions as memory limitations, distractions, shifts of attention and interest, and errors (random or characteristic) in applying his knowledge of the language in actual performance. . . . We thus make a fundamental distinction between *competence* (the speaker-hearer's knowledge of his language) and *performance* (the actual use of language in concrete situations)." [15, p.3-4]

this [knowledge] even when we are unable to detect what it entails in concrete cases." [20, p.10]

There is no place for a principled distinction between competence and performance in an adequate theory of human language. There is simply human language itself, exactly as it is and how it operates. Its capacities are certainly limited, but those limits cannot rationally be said to be an independent object of study. It may be impaired by disease or injury. It may operate nondeterministically, at different times mapping the same input into different outputs. But it cannot rationally be said to make errors, because an error in performance exists only with respect to an expectation about performance. The language module does not have any expectations about its own performance. A performance error, then, is merely an incorrect expectation about performance, arising from an inadequate theory of language. A theory of performance errors is therefore inherently incoherent.

Our proposed framework — that human language is the process of constructing linguistic representations of extralinguistic information — clarifies what form the theory of human language must take. Human language *is* the unitary language computation f itself, exactly as it is and how it operates. By equating comprehension and production in a fundamental manner, the framework says that it is not possible to talk of a model of language comprehension in isolation from production and acquisition, simply because these processes cannot be separated. All are manifestations of the one unitary language process, that of continually constructing linguistic representations of the instantaneous extralinguistic information. An adequate model of language comprehension would necessarily be an adequate model of production (and acquisition as well).

Again, it is important to stress that our proposed interpretation is a conceptual framework for addressing scientific questions, not a computational theory of human language itself. The substantive answers to these puzzles lie in particular computational theories of human language. In section 6.3 below we review the technical results obtained in chapters 2 through 5, and in prior work. These results are concrete technical contributions to the computational theory of human language.

6.1.2 The Parsing of E-Languages

Here we briefly consider the implications of our proposed interpretation of human language for the field of computational linguistics. Computational linguistics is concerned with the engineering problem of designing computer systems that involve human language, such as machine translation systems and natural-language interfaces to database query systems. A central component of current computational linguistics technology is the parser.

A parser is an algorithm that assigns structural descriptions to linguistic expressions, according to a model of language that is typically represented as a formal grammar. The input to a parser is an expression and a grammar, and the output is a set of structural descriptions for that expression according to that grammar. An expression is a string of abstract symbols (typically the orthographic forms of words, occasionally the orthographic forms of morphemes) that is intended to model, albeit in a highly-idealized manner, the linguistic sensation. A grammar is finite description of a (potentially infinite) set of structural descriptions, each of which yields a linguistic expression. We say that the (formal) language of the grammar is the set of linguistic expressions that are the yield of some structural description enumerated by the grammar.[3]

Grammars are evaluated by the criterion of descriptive adequacy. A grammar must describe exactly (that is, enumerate all and only) the possible structural descriptions of a given human language. Each structural description must describe a possible linguistic interpretation of the expression whose yield it is, and each humanly-possible linguistic interpretation of a given expression must be represented by a structural description of the grammar.

Parsers are evaluated by three criteria: computational efficiency, implementation correctness, and psychological accuracy. A parser is evaluated as an algorithm is, by the twin criterion of efficiency and correctness. The efficiency of a parser is the (worst case) amount of time and space required to output a set of structural descriptions for a given input expression, according to a given input grammar. The output set of structural descriptions may be represented in a compact manner, pro-

---

[3]Recall Chomsky's [20] distinction between E(xternalized)-language and I(nternalized)-language. E-language is language as an externalized object, as a set of linguistic expressions (perhaps) paired with their structural descriptions. I-language is language as an internalized object, as a set of linguistic representations paired with their cognitive correlates. A parser computes a mapping from linguistic expressions to structural descriptions, and therefore parsing inherently belongs to the E-language perspective. From an I-language perspective, parsing verges on the incoherent, being entirely irrelevant to human language computations. From an E-language perspective, however, parsing is a central language computation.

vided that membership queries for that compact set representation may be computed very efficiently. A parser is correct if it assigns to every input expression exactly the structural descriptions whose yield is the input expression (according to the grammar).

Given our current understanding of nondeterminism, the NP-hardness of the unitary language computation means that correct natural language parsers will require an exponentially-increasing amount of time to parse expressions of linearly-increasing length. In short, parsers are inherently intractable. This empirical consequence is nothing new; it is well-known that natural language parsers that assign nontrivial structural descriptions to linguistic expressions require time that increases exponentially in the size of their input grammar and expression.

A parser is also evaluated in relation to human performance. That is, the input/output behavior of a parser must also be psychologically accurate. Most expressions of a natural language are highly ambiguous when considered in isolation, and hence they will be assigned multiple structural descriptions by a parser, one "parse" for each possible linguistic interpretation of that expression. Each of these interpretations will be more or less salient to human language users. In general, the number of possible interpretations for an expression increases exponentially in the size of the expression, although language users are typically conscious of only one of these exponentially-many interpretations. Therefore, in order for a parser to be useful for practical purposes, it must accurately order the structural descriptions that it outputs according to their psychological saliency. The accuracy of a parser is given by how well the order that it assigns to its output structural descriptions agrees with the order assigned by human language users.

Unfortunately, it will not be possible for parsers (as they are conventionally understood) to be accurate. According to our proposed interpretation of human language, the input to language comprehension is extralinguistic information, and the output is a linguistic representation of that extralinguistic information. The extralinguistic information includes sensations, intentions, beliefs, models of agents, the mental lexicon, the conceptual system, and so forth. A linguistic expression, which is an idealized sensation, is but a small portion of this extralinguistic information. It is the totality of the extralinguistic information that determines a unique output linguistic representation for the process of language comprehension. When the input to a parser (an expression and a grammar) contains so much less information than is available to the language user, then ambiguities in the parser output will inevitably increase at an exponential rate. These global ambiguities cannot be accurately ordered by means of a fixed prior distribution on the set of structural descriptions, simply because the extralinguistic information available to the human language user is constantly changing, and hence cannot be accurately modeled by a fixed distribution. The input to a parser must also contain far less computationally-accessible information than is available to the human language user, and therefore a parser will encounter intractability even when the language user does not.

No published parser includes a grammar that even remotely approaches descriptive adequacy for any natural language. However, even if such a descriptively-adequate parser were constructed, it would not be possible for that parser to accurately or efficiently reproduce the linguistic behavior of the language user, simply because parsing (as it is conventionally understood) is an inaccurate characterization of the logical problem of language comprehension. This implication of our proposed intepretation of human language should not be surprising, because the inaccuracy, intractability, and descriptive inadequacy of existing parsers is well-known by practitioners, although very little discussed.

6.2 The Complexity Thesis

We have argued that the computations of human language are bounded above and below by nondeterministic polynomial time (that is, they are NP-complete). In this section we review the implications of placing human language in the abstract hierarchy of computational complexity, and discuss the significance of proving an NP-hard lower bound on language computations. The consequences of our complexity thesis, that language is NP-complete, are both practical and theoretical.

One consequence of our complexity thesis is to offer a new (and very different) perspective on human language, where things previously obscured now become clear. By placing human language in the much-studied complexity hierarchy, we better understand its overall computational structure, by analogy to the other equivalent combinatorial problems in its complexity class. We see that language computations are not like two-person zero-sum games of perfect information (PSPACE), nor are they like pointer-following (LSPACE) or directed search in a feasible space of possibilities ($\mathcal{P}$). Rather, human language is like blind search in an exponentially large space ($\mathcal{NP}$), to find efficient witnesses. (Recall that an efficient witness for a given input is a short, easily-verified proof that the input should be accepted. In our case, the input is extralinguistic information, and the efficient witness is a linguistic representation of that information.)

We may also ask, what are the implications of the $\mathcal{NP}$ lower bounds for theories of language processing?

A theory of language processing is an explicit computational model of the language user, that attempts to explain (or at least describe) the comprehension, production, and acquisition of languages. Sometimes such a theory is called a performance theory, or a theory of sentence processing. The unspoken question that currently defines this field of psycholinguistics is, roughly, to explain why human linguistic performance is so bad, given the inherent simplicity of the language processing task. We argue that this formulation of the research question is misguided, on two grounds.

First, if language computations are indeed NP-complete, as we have argued they are, then the central research question is to explain the unexpected achievements of human linguistic performance, not their limits. The central open research question is to explain why human linguistic performance is so sucessful, given the inherent complexity of the language processing task and our sustained failure to design efficient, descriptively-adequate systems for natural language processing.

Second, the complexity proofs in this monograph strongly suggest that the relation between competence and performance, between a generative linguistic theory and a theory of language processing, is not one of limited ability. This fact is contrary to the frequently expressed and widely held beliefs of theoretical linguists, psychologists, cognitive scientists, and computational linguists. To sample but a small portion of the more influential published work expressing this widely-espoused view, see [8, 15, 20, 24, 45, 68, 69, 72, 89]. If linguistic performance really were the limited ability to use linguistic competence, then two consequences would naturally accrue. The first is that language users would have difficulty processing those utterances that are truly computationally difficult. The second is that language users should not have difficulty processing computationally trivial utterances.

There are infinite classes of utterances that may be easily parsed (that is, assigned correct structural descriptions by a simple and very fast algorithm), yet these utterances are extremely difficult for language users to process. One such class is those utterances containing pronouns that result in trivial obviation graphs, such as complete or edge-free obviation graphs. Such utterances contain anaphoric elements that are either all mutually obviative, or all not obviative. Computing the referential dependencies for such utterances is computationally trivial, yet language users cannot do it. In fact, they appear to have difficulty processing utterances with multiple antecedents, regardless of the obviation relations involved. A second instance is garden path sentences, such as *The horse raced past the barn fell*, which are quickly parsed by simple algorithms, yet seem difficult for language users to process.

There are also infinite classes of complex expressions that cannot be efficiently parsed by any known algorithm, yet these sentences are processed effortlessly by human language users. One such class is expressions containing many local ambiguities, such as lexically ambiguous words. Nearly every linguistic expression is in this class, and language users rarely have any difficulty processing them. However, such expressions sorely tax the performance of current parsers, because it is not known how to correctly resolve lexical ambiguities locally, without building a complete structural description and thereby being forced to examine an exponential number of possible parses. A second instance is utterances understood as containing phonologically empty elements (so-called empty categories, such as traces or PRO). These empty categories represent some aspect of the language user's knowledge of his language, and therefore they must in some way be detected and represented by a descriptively-adequate parser, either explicitly or implicitly. Detecting empty categories and computing their antecedents is effortless for humans, but so extremely difficult for current parsing technology that most practitioners choose to ignore the problem entirely.

It is not at all surprising that attempts to explain so-called "performance limitations" as resource-bounded competence have all failed so miserably. One fixed resource bound has never been subtle enough to capture any diverse range of observed linguistic phenomena. In order to have explanatory force, a small number of resource bounds must be postulated to explain a large number of seemingly unrelated performance limitations. To postulate a different resource bound for every construction is merely to restate the performance facts. To my knowledge, no one has even tried to explain a truly diverse range of performance facts—say from the phonology and syntax, or involving both referential dependencies and phrase structure—using one resource bound. Nor has anyone successfully described even a similar set of performance facts using one resource bound. This may be seen in oft-cited work of Miller and Chomsky [72], who attempted to calculate a numerical bound on the depth of acceptable recursive phrase structure embeddings. Their work only served to demonstrate that no fixed bound could be found for the handful of constructions that they examined, even in in the limited domain of English phrase structure computations. A second example comes from the numerous failed attempts to explain garden pathing as the inability to properly resolve a local ambiguity in phrase structure attachment. The central difficulty in such an endeavor is to explain why some types of local ambiguity exhaust computational resources, while many others don't, and why global ambiguities (which must always be more costly) do not. It is not currently known how to resolve such inconsistencies.

Even worse, an account in terms of resource limitations has never been plausibly motivated, that is, shown remotely relevant to human language processing. A theory of resource utilization makes exactly one fundamental prediction: that the resource-consuming process must for some input at some critical point in the computation exhaust the available resources, at which point the computational process will terminate with disastrous consequences. Those inputs that exceed the critical point will be *de facto* rejected, even though they are virtually identical to other inputs that do not exceed the critical point and are accepted. Therefore, in order to demonstrate the plausibility of an explanation in terms of resource limits, someone must exhibit similar linguistic inputs on both sides of such a critical point. Such a critical point has never even been discussed in the performance literature, let alone demonstrated.

Nor can performance limitations be explained as errors in competence, contra Chomsky [15]. The language device cannot rationally be said to make systematic or pervasive errors, because such errors can exist only with respect to a designer's intentions or goals, and the language device was not designed. Systematic "errors" cannot therefore be errors in performance, only empirical inadequacies of a particular theory of linguistic competence. A true error in performance must be intermittent and unexpected. And if, as is widely-assumed, such errors are not to be accounted for by the competence theory, then they cannot logically constitute evidence for or against the competence theory. This is exactly the *a priori* segregation of evidence into "relevant" and "irrelevant" that Chomsky [17, 20] has so powerfully argued against. Empirical evidence for or against a scientific theory might in principle be found anywhere. Linguistics is no different: the one scientific theory of human language must explain performance errors, because such errors are relevant evidence for the theory [50, 92]. Language errors cannot have their own scientific theory. To see this, examine [5], which argues that the independent tiers of the autosegmental model can explain facts about speech errors, such as the fact that the stress contour of a sentence remains unchanged when vowels, syllables, parts of syllables, or even whole words are substituted or transposed in that sentence.

6.3 The Language Complexity Game

We have proposed a novel methodology for investigating human language computations, called the language complexity game. This is an adversarial game played between two abstract players, where one player attempts to establish that language computations are more complex than previously thought, and the other player attempts to establish that language computations are less complex that previously thought. Each turn in the game consists of a critique of current understanding and an improved model of human language. The ultimate outcome of this game is a computational theory of human language that accurately captures the computationally significant aspects of human language.

In this concluding section, we compare the technical results achieved by our proposed method to those achieved by generative linguistics. To do this, we discuss in detail how each of the technical results in the preceeding chapters (chapters 2 to 5) contributed to our understanding of human language, and why these results are not the expected outcome of an investigation within the generative framework.

6.3.1 Methodological Suggestions

In the computational study of human language, the central research question is to precisely explain the comprehension, production, and acquisition of human language. This reduces to the central empirical question of understanding the unitary language computation $f(i, M) = \langle r, M' \rangle$, and the derivative questions, of understanding the possible linguistic representations r, the set M of representations possible in a particular human language, the set $\mathcal{M}$ of possible human languages (the universal grammar), and the distribution and structure of extralinguistic information. A research result is a precise, empirically-motivated description of a human language computation at some level of abstraction. (In the body of this monograph, we describe language computations in the most abstract manner, as computational problems. In general, less abstract descriptions are increasingly difficult to motivate and will require more supporting empirical argumentation.) The methodology of our language complexity game focuses research efforts on the computationally-significant aspects of human language.

In the generative study of human language, the central research question is to precisely characterize the language user's knowledge of language. This reduces to the empirical question of understanding how linguistic knowledge is represented. The outcome of such an investigation is a finite description of an infinite set of linguistic representations (that is, a theory of universal grammar $\mathcal{M}$). A research result is an explicit finite description of a set of empirically-motivated representations for some natural class of linguistic knowledge. The methodology of generative linguistics focuses research efforts on obtaining descriptions that are elegant.

The generative approach has revolutionized our understanding of human language, and yielded a long list of impressive technical results. Our technical results — which consist primarily of precise, empirically-motivated descriptions of human language computations — would not be possible without the prior work of generative linguists. However, the computational approach that we have proposed complements the generative approach in one respect, and improves on it in another crucial respect.

As we mentioned above, the methodology of generative linguistics favors linguistic theories whose finite description is compact and elegant. What is not so often mentioned is that a linguistic theory can only be compact and elegant with respect to some chosen formal language of descriptions, called a description language [34, 96]. (A *description language* is a formal language within which a formal theory is described or specified.) If the description language were changed, then generative theories that were formerly compact and elegant, may no longer be so, and vice-versa. We argue that this approach is therefore somewhat misguided, and that it will favor certain empirical discoveries over other discoveries that are arguably more important to our understanding of language.

By favoring elegant theories, generative linguistics in effect reduces the question of understanding the universal grammar ($\mathcal{M}$) to the question of understanding that component of the universal grammar that can be described compactly and elegantly in the chosen description language. Just as this approach will favor certain discoveries, it will also disfavor other crucial discoveries, including those that are computationally significant. We present concrete examples of this scientific bias below in section 6.3.2. This bias is certainly unfortunate if we believe that human language is a computational system, and must therefore also hold that its computational properties are of central scientific importance.

This bias towards compact and elegant descriptions in a chosen description language is misguided. For one, the chosen description language of modern generative linguistics has never (to our knowledge) been discussed in a substantive manner in the published literature, let alone made explicit or justified on scientific grounds.[4] It is difficult to see how a description language (when it is finally proposed) can be falsified: no known empirical evidence bears directly on the properties of the description language for generative linguistic theories, and the indirect evidence is so slender as to be intangible. Thus, the chosen description language can only be ad-hoc at best and not subject to scientific investigation at worst. Two, even if a particular description language could be made explicit and motivated empirically, there is no reason to believe that the innate universal grammar or any particular language must be compactly described within that description language.

---

[4]This observation is certainly true for ongoing approaches to linguistics (post late 1970s), including principle-and-parameter approaches as well as nonlinear phonological theory and prosodic morphology. Although *The Sound Pattern of English* (SPE) [23] is not a part of current generative linguisitcs, it does appear to propose an explicit description language for phonological models. In that work, Chomsky and Halle stated an explicit evaluation metric for phonological grammars, which some might construe as a description language for phonological theory. However, their proposed evaluation metric has nontrival empirical problems [51, 52] and some technical problems as well [85], and it is not known how to repair it's empirical defects. More importantly, the SPE description language for the phonological grammars of particular languages cannot reasonably be considered a description langauge for phonological theories, of which SPE is but one.

It is crucial not to confuse this question, of how generative linguistic theories are to be represented, with the related question of how each M and the $\mathcal{M}$ are represented in the language user. While the former question is of dubious scientific interest, the latter question is an empirical question of undisputable scientific interest (see section 1.3.1).

Recall that M is the set of linguistic representations permissible in a given language, and that each member of M represents the language user's linguistic knowledge about some extralinguistic information. The universal grammar $\mathcal{M}$ is the set of such M. Although there is little or no known empirical evidence bearing on how these sets are characterized constructively in the language user, the empirical evidence bearing on each M in extension (as a set of linguistic representations) and on $\mathcal{M}$ in extension (as a set of such sets) is very strong and readily available. For example, we might question the language user about his linguistic knowledge of extralinguistic information. If the language user answers our questions, then he must internally represent the linguistic information needed to answer to our questions. Therefore, it is much more important that the universal grammar $\mathcal{M}$ and its members (sets of linguistic representations permissible in a given language) be described accurately and comprehensively (in extension, as well as in intension) than this description be elegant or compact in some ad-hoc description language.

The outcome of the language complexity game is a set of precise, empirically-motivated problem statements that are accurate and comprehensive in computationally-significant respects. Each problem statement describes a class of language computations at the highest level of computational abstraction, as a relation between inputs and outputs. (In this monograph, our problem statements were presented in two parts, a detailed language model and a broad problem statement, that only result in a precise problem statement when they are combined.) There is no concern that these computational problems be elegantly or compactly described, only that they be accurate and comprehensive in computationally significant respects.

To summarize, our proposed methodology is preferred over the methods of generative linguistics for two reasons. First, if we hold that human language is a computational system, as many prominent linguists do, then we must also hold that the computational properties and structures of human language are of greater scientific importance than the elegance of our linguistic theories, which favors our proposed methodology over the methods of generative linguistics.[5] Second, if we accept that a particular human language is a particular computing machine performing the unitary language computation f_M from extralinguistic information to an infinite set M of linguistic representations, then a generative procedure that enumerates the same set M is an externalized view of the language user, that cannot possibly be a scientific theory of how the sets M or $\mathcal{M}$ are finitely characterized in the language user.

Let us next consider concrete examples. In section 6.3.2, we review some of our technical contributions to the study of human language, and explain why these results are not the likely outcome of an generative linguistics investigation. Our discussion is directed more to the student of language than to the student of computation.

6.3.2 Technical Contributions to Linguistics

A technical contribution to the computational theory of human language consists of a precise, empirically-motivated description of some class of language computations. In this monograph, we have couched our descriptions at the highest level of abstraction, as computational problems, and formulated our problem statements within the context of a language complexity game. Here we review our technical contributions, relate them to the study of language, and compare them to technical results obtained in generative linguistics.

Beginning with chapter 2, we investigated the language user's knowledge of anaphora. We established that the language user has conscious knowledge of antecedence (that an anaphoric element obtains its mental reference from another linguistic element) and obviation (that two linguistic elements cannot share any mental referents). The central research question regarding knowledge of anaphora is: (1) What referential dependencies are possible in a given language? Two related questions are: (2) What instrinsic properties must two linguistic elements have in order to be coreferential? and (3) What is the correspondence between referential dependences and other linguistic and extralinguistic information?

Although all three questions are crucial to understanding the language

---

[5]Many prominent linguists have explicitly proposed to view human language as a computational system, including Chomsky [17, 20, 21], although few have then proposed to study its computational properties.

user's knowledge of anaphora, and hence central to the enterprise of generative linguistics, only the third question as been an active research topic in generative linguistics. Moreover, generative researchers have confined their attention to a small portion of the correspondence between referential dependencies and cognitive information. Let us briefly consider this prior work.

Prior work has concentrated almost exclusively on the syntactically-determined distribution of coreference relations. The central (collective) result is the *Binding Theory*, which attempts to elegantly specify the correspondence between relations of the phrase structure (such as immediate domination and c-command) and relations of referential dependency (in particular, obviation and immediate antecedence). We represent relations of referential dependency by means of a labeled directed graph, called the graph of referential dependencies, or RDG. The classic binding theory contains three conditions — Conditions A, B, and C — each of which maps properties of the phrase structure into properties of the RDG. It is widely assumed (with some known exceptions, such as split antecedence for plural pronouns in English) that two elements may be coreferential only if they agree on all agreement features, where "agree" is taken to mean "their features do not disagree."

The Binding Theory does not completely specify the mapping from phrase structures to referential dependencies. For example, Condition A states that a reflexive or reciprocal α must have an immediate antecedent β, and that α and β must participate in a certain phrase structure relation R. However, the fact that some anaphoric element α and some element β participate in the relation R does not imply that β is the immediate antecedent of α, simply because there may be another element γ that also satisfies the condition A. In short, condition A does not determine a unique mapping from relations of phrase structure to relations of referential dependency. The same is true for the other conditions. Condition B states that a pronoun α must obviate certain other elements in the phrase structure. Although Condition B uniquely determines a portion of the obviation relations involving α, it says nothing about antecedence relations involving the pronoun α. Likewise, Condition C states that a referring-expression δ must obviate certain other elements in the phrase structure, but does not specify which anaphoric elements have δ as their antecedent.

In short, generative linguistics has restricted its attention to a small portion of the total information necessary to compute the referential dependencies of linguistic representation. In doing this, they have mostly ignored questions (1) and (2) above.

Question (2) is the agreement condition, namely, what intrinsic properties must an anaphoric element α and a referring-expression β have in order for β to be the antecedent of α? Clearly the nature of the agreement condition is a central empirical question about referential dependencies. The widely-accepted answer (the standard agreement condition, or SAC) is that α and β each have certain intrinsic properties, including agreement features, and that β can be the antecedent of α only if α and β do not disagree on any agreement feature. In section 3.2, the maximizer proved that the Anaphora Problem was NP-hard according to the SAC, which establishes that the exact nature of the agreement condition is a computationally significant issue in human language. In section 3.3, the minimizer falsified nearly every prediction of the SAC and proposed an alternative agreement condition (the Anaphoric Uniqueness Condition, or AUC). The ease with which nearly every prediction of the SAC was falsified strongly suggests that the agreement condition was not hithertofore the subject of serious empirical investigation. This seems peculiar, given that it is central to our understanding of the language user's knowledge of anaphora.

The most important question about anaphora, which has been largely neglected by generative linguistics, is question (1): What referential dependencies are possible in a given language? An answer to this question in the generative framework is a finite procedure that enumerates the sets of obviation and immediate antecedence relations possible in a given language. Although this question would seem to be central to the generative investigation of anaphora, as far as we know, no generative linguist has explicitly addressed it. At best, this question has been considered indirectly and incompletely, in terms of possible phrase structures and possible mappings from phrase structures to referential dependencies (via the Binding Theory). Even if the Binding Theory completely specified the mapping from phrase structures to referential dependencies in a given language, which it does not, it would still not constitute even an indirect answer to this question, simply because we would also need to exactly enumerate the possible phrase structures of the language along with all the other linguistic and extralinguistic information needed to uniquely determine the referential dependencies in a given (partial) linguistic representation.

In the language complexity game, this central question (1) about the space of possible referential dependencies must be investigated, simply because computations involving anaphora are a significant (and computationally complex) part of the unitary language computation.

In chapter 5 we considered the interaction between referential dependencies and syntactic ellipsis. We established that the language user has knowledge of the covariant and invariant intepretations of an ellipsed anaphoric element. The central research question about syntactic ellipsis is how elliptical structures are represented in the language user. A related question is what referential dependencies are possible for an elliptical structure, and how those dependencies relate to other referential dependencies.

These questions have been studied extensively in generative linguistics, with considerable success. As but one small example, our function-sharing model of ellipsis is based on an idea due to generative linguists, that the overt and ellipsed VPs in a VP-ellipsis construction correspond to identical predicates. However, it is equally true that generative linguists have strongly advocated the copy model of ellipsis (as recently as last year [53]), which is based on the fundamentally incorrect idea that the ellipsed VP in a VP-ellipsis construction is an explicit copy of the overt VP. According to the methods of generative linguisitics, neither the copy model nor the function-sharing model is clearly preferred. One model allows more elegant descriptions for certain phenomena, and the other model does for other phenomena.[6] Each has its own empirical flaws. In the generative framework, the choice between the two models is largely a toss-up.

In our proposed framework, however, the choice between the two models is clear. First, the maximizer proved that the Anaphora Problem in the copy model is PSPACE-hard. Next, the minimizer demonstrated that ellipsed referential dependencies had none of the properties associated with a copy operation or with a PSPACE-hard computation. A

---

[6]Some might even argue that the copy model is inherently more elegant, because it reduces the research problem of explaining ellipsis to the research problem of explaining all other linguistic phenomena. Thus, the copy model appears to solve ellipsis in one simple reduction step. In this view, the function-sharing model is not nearly so elegant, because it consists of substantive theoretical statements about ellipsis, such as a generalization of the link relation and a revision of the binding conditions.

copy operation predicts that the original and its copy are fundamentally independent. Yet referential dependencies in the ellipsed VP are equivalent to those in the overt VP. A PSPACE-hard computation corresponds to a branching computation tree, that includes existential branches as well as universal branches. Yet there is nothing in the computation of referential dependencies in an ellipsed constituent that remotely suggests a branching computation tree with universal branches. The large jump from the $\mathcal{NP}$ computation of the function-sharing model to the PSPACE computation of the copy model is simply not justified by the facts of ellipsis. The copy model has absolutely no motivation or scientific basis in a computational framework.

Let us step back from the fray for the moment. As impartial students of language, whose sole goal is to understand human language, which result should we prefer? Should we prefer no bias or a strong bias for the function-sharing model?

If we believe that human language is a computational system, then we must also believe that the computational properties of that system are of paramount importance. There is such a chasm between the computational properties of the copy model and those of the function-sharing model, that one must be flat wrong. Although the copy model may have a certain intuitive appeal or simple-minded elegance, its computational properties have no empirical justification. The ellipsed VP has none of the intrinsic properties of a copied object, such as independence from its original with respect to linguistically important properties. Moreover, the unitary language computation for anaphora has none of the abstract properties of a PSPACE-complete computation. The embeded ellipsed VPs of a recursive ellipsis construction in no sense correspond to alternating players in a zero-sum game. Therefore, if we believe that language is a computational system, then we cannot rationally continue to consider the copy model (or any of its variants) a plausible model of ellipsis.

A Background

This appendix reviews the mathematical background necessary to appreciate our technical results. We review the mathematical theory of computational complexity in section A.1 and define the computational problems employed in our reductions in section A.2.

A.1 Overview of Computational Complexity Theory

This section introduces the powerful theory of computational complexity. Computational complexity theory measures the intrinsic lower-bound difficulty of obtaining the solution to a computational problem no matter how the solution is obtained. It classifies these problems according to the amount of computational resources (in our case, time and space) needed to solve them on a deterministic Turing machine.

A computational problem is a precisely-stated relationship between inputs and their corresponding outputs. For example, the *Factoring Problem* is stated as: given a positive integer as input, output its prime factors. With few exceptions, every computational problem has two variants. In the *constructive* variant, we are required to provide a constructive solution to the problem. In the *decision* variant, we are only require to say whether a solution exists or not. A decision problem corresponding to the Factoring Problem is the *Composite Number Problem*: decide whether a given positive integer may be factored into two positive integers greater than 1. In the next section, section A.2, we explicitly define the problems used in our reductions.

A.1.1 Complexity is a function of input size

Computational problems are solved by algorithms; algorithms run on computers; computers consume computational resources, such as time or space. Therefore, the complexity of a problem is given indirectly by the algorithms that solve it.

The complexity of an algorithm is the rate at which it consumes the computational resources of time and space, expressed as the order of growth of a function in the size of the problem input. Orders of growth are an upper bound on the resource requirements of an algorithm. They are useful because they abstract from many irrelevant details of the computer.

Algorithm complexity provides an upper bound on problem complexity: the most efficient known algorithm for a problem gives the tightest upper bound. Problem complexity can also be bounded from below by a reduction, according to the theory of computational complexity.

A.1.2 Three Important Complexity Classes

A complexity class is that set of computational problems that can be solved in a given amount of a given computational resource on a given computing machine. The two most widely-studied computational resources are deterministic time and space, that is, time and space on a deterministic Turing machine. This monograph refers to three complexity classes: $\mathcal{P}$, $\mathcal{NP}$, and PSPACE. These classes are defined algebraically as follows.

$\mathcal{P}$ is the natural and important class of problems solvable in deterministic $\mathcal{P}$olynomial time, that is, on a deterministic Turing machine within time n^j for some integer j, where n denotes the size of the problem to be solved. Problems must be encoded in a "reasonable" way for a size measure to make sense (for discussion, see [31]). $\mathcal{P}$ is considered to be the class of problems that can be solved efficiently. For example, sorting takes $n \cdot \log n$ time in the worst case using a variety of algorithms, and therefore is efficiently solvable.

$\mathcal{NP}$ is the class of all problems solvable in $\mathcal{N}$ondeterministic $\mathcal{P}$olynomial time, that is, using a polynomial amount of time on a nondeterministic Turing machine. Informally, a problem is in $\mathcal{NP}$ if one can guess an answer to the problem and then verify its correctness in polynomial time. For example, the problem of deciding whether a whole number i is composite is in $\mathcal{NP}$ because it can be solved by guessing a pair of potential divisors, and then quickly checking if their product equals i. $\mathcal{NP}$ contains $\mathcal{P}$, although it is not known if the containment is proper.

Finally, *PSPACE* is the class of problems solvable in deterministic polynomial *space*. PSPACE contains $\mathcal{NP}$ because polynomial space allows us to simulate an entire $\mathcal{NP}$ computation, but it is not known if the inclusion is proper. Intuitively, PSPACE is the class of combinatorial two-person games: it includes the problems of winning generalized versions of Checkers, Go, and Parker Brothers' Instant Insanity. Many problems in formal language theory are known to be PSPACE-complete, such as context-sensitive language recognition and finite state automaton inequivalence and intersection.

A.1.3 Establishing Complexity Classifications

We say a problem T is $\mathcal{C}$-*hard* if T is at least as hard computationally as any problem in the complexity class $\mathcal{C}$. Note that T need not be in $\mathcal{C}$ to be $\mathcal{C}$-hard. A problem is $\mathcal{C}$-*complete* if it is both $\mathcal{C}$-hard and included included in the complexity class $\mathcal{C}$.

Complexity classifications are established with the proof technique of reduction. A *reduction* converts instances of a problem T of known complexity into instances of a problem S whose complexity we wish to determine (written $T \leq_{\mathcal{P}} S$). The reduction operates in polynomial time. Therefore, if we had a polynomial time algorithm for solving S, then we could also solve T in polynomial time, simply by converting instances of T into S. (This follows because the composition of two polynomial time functions is also polynomial time, provided T cannot itself be solved in polynomial time.) For example, if we choose T to be NP-complete, then the polynomial time reduction shows that S is at least as hard as T, or NP-hard. If we were also to prove that S was in $\mathcal{NP}$, then S would be NP-complete.

NP-complete problems can be solved only by methods too slow for even the fastest computers. Since it is widely believed, though not proved, that no faster methods of solution can ever be found for these problems, NP-complete problems are considered the easiest computationally intractable problems. famous NP-complete problem is the *Traveling Salesman Problem*, that is, to find the shortest route for a traveling salesman who must visit a number of cities and return to the original starting point.

For additional details, the reader is urged to refer to [4], which introduces the theory of computational complexity and explores the relationship between computational complexity and natural language formalisms. For an excellent reference work for the theory of computational complexity, see [31].

A.2 Some Problem Definitions

In this section, we explicitly define the computational problems that we use in our reductions. There are three such problems: Graph Coloring, 3SAT, and QBF. Let us consider each in turn.

Graphs A graph $G = \langle V, E \rangle$ consists of a finite set V of vertices and E of edges. Each edge (v_i, v_j) in the set E is a relation between the vertices v_i and v_j in V (written $E \subseteq V \times V$, or $E \subseteq \{(v_i, v_j) : v_i \in V, v_j \in V\}$). We say two vertices v_i and v_j are *incident* in the graph $G = \langle V, E \rangle$ if and only if $(v_i, v_j) \in E$.

This set-theoretic representation of a graph is often not very illuminating. Therefore, we will often depict the vertices of a graph as points, and the edges of a graph as line segments between points depicting the appropriate vertices.

The *Graph k-Coloring Problem* (also called the Chromatic Number Problem) is to color the vertices of a graph using k distinct colors in such a way that vertices connected by an edge (that is, vertices incident to each other) must have different colors. This is equivalent to the Map Coloring Problem, where adjacent areas of the map must receive different colors. We may state the Graph k-Coloring Problem precisely as follows. The input is a graph $G = \langle V, E \rangle$ and a set $C = \{1, 2, \ldots, k\}$ of colors. The output is k-coloring f of G, that is, a total function $f : V \to C$ such that $(v_i, v_j) \in V \Rightarrow f(v_i) \neq f(v_j)$. The corresponding decision problem is to decide if a given graph has a k-coloring.

This problem is NP-complete (Karp, [48]) for any fixed $k \geq 3$, and remains so for many restricted classes of graphs, such as planar graphs [31, p.191].

Boolean Logic What is the Boolean logic? A Boolean *variable* is a logical variable that is restricted to the values '0' and '1', which are understood as meaning `false` and `true`, respectively. A *truth assignment* for a given set $X = \{x_1, x_2, \ldots, x_m\}$ of Boolean variables is a function $t : X \to \{0, 1\}$ that assigns a truth value to every variable in U.

A *literal* is an instance of a variable, that may be negated or not. Negation reverses truth values. That is, the positive literal x of the variable x is true under t if and only if the variable x is true under t. The negative literal $\bar{x}$ of the variable x is true if and only if the variable x is false under t.

A *clause* is a set of literals combined with an implicit disjunction. That is, a clause over X is *satisfied* by a truth assignment t to X if and only if at least one of its literals is true under t; otherwise, the clause is false.

A collection of clauses is a set of clauses combined with an implicit

Background

conjunction. That is, a collection C of clauses is *satisfied* by a truth assignment t if and only if every clause in C is satisfied by t. (Such a collection of clauses is called a Boolean formula in Conjunctive Normal Form.) We say that such a collection of clauses is *satisfiable* if and only if there exists some truth assignment t that satisfies every clause in that collection.

The famous *Satisfiability Problem* (SAT) is to find a truth assignment that satisfies a given collection of Boolean clauses. The input is a set X of Boolean variables and a collection $C = \{C_1, C_2, \ldots, C_k\}$ of Boolean clauses over X. The output is a truth assignment t that satisfies every clause in C. The corresponding decision problem is to decide if such a satisfying truth assignment exists.

The *3-Satisfiability Problem* (3SAT) is a restricted variant of the Satisfiablity Problem where the input Boolean clauses $C_1, C_2, \ldots, C_k$ each contain exactly 3 literals. Such a collection of 3-clauses is called a "Boolean formula in 3-conjunctive normal form."

A *quantified Boolean formula* is a collection of clauses over the Boolean variables $X = \{x_1, x_2, \ldots, x_m\}$, quantified by a sequence of those variables:

$$Q_1 x_1 Q_2 x_2 \ldots Q_m x_m \{C_1, C_2, \ldots, C_k\} \qquad (A.2.1)$$

Each quantifier Q_i may be existential ($\exists$) or universal ($\forall$).

Let $C = \{C_1, C_2, \ldots, C_k\}$ be a collection of clauses. Then $C[x = v]$ is a new collection of clauses, with the variable x assigned the truth value v in C (a truth value is either '0' or '1'). That is, all literals of x in C are replaced by the constants '0' or '1' in $C[x = v]$, depending on the value v and the polarity of the literal.

A quantified Boolean formula Ω of the form

$$Q_1 x_1 Q_2 x_2 \ldots Q_m x_m C$$

may be true or false, according to the following recursive rules. If $Q_1 = \exists$, then Ω is true if and only if either $(Q_2 x_2 \ldots Q_m x_m C[x_1 = 0])$ *or* $(Q_2 x_2 \ldots Q_m x_m C[x_1 = 1])$ is true. Otherwise, $Q_1 = \forall$, and then Ω is true if and only if $(Q_2 x_2 \ldots Q_m x_m C[x_1 = 0])$ is true and $(Q_2 x_2 \ldots Q_m x_m C[x_1 = 1])$ is true as well.

The *Quantified Boolean Formula Problem* (QBF) is to decide if a given quantified Boolean formula is true or false. The input is a quantified

Boolean formula in the form (A.2.1). The output is 'yes' if and only if the formula is true. This problem is PSPACE-complete [98].

Bibliography

[1] G. Alvarez, B. Brodie, and T. McCoy, editors. *Proceedings of the First Eastern States Conference on Linguistics.* Ohio State University, Columbus, OH, 1984. (Includes special session on agreement.).
[2] S. Anderson. *A-morphous Morphology.* Cambridge University Press, Cambridge, 1992.
[3] M. Barlow and C. A. Ferguson, editors. *Agreement in Natural Language: Approaches, Theories, Descriptions.* CSLI, Stanford, 1988.
[4] G. E. Barton, R. C. Berwick, and E. S. Ristad. *Computational Complexity and Natural Language.* MIT Press, Cambridge, 1987.
[5] D. Becker. Speech error evidence for autosegmental levels. *Linguistic Inquiry*, 10(1):165–167, 1979.
[6] R. Berwick. Computational complexity and lexical functional grammar. *American Journal of Computational Linguistics*, 8(3-4):97–109, 1982.
[7] R. Berwick. *The Acquisition of Syntactic Knowledge.* MIT Press, Cambridge, 1985.
[8] R. Berwick and A. Weinberg. *The Grammatical Basis of Linguistic Performance: Language Use and Acquisition.* MIT Press, Cambridge, 1984.
[9] R. Berwick and A. Weinberg. Deterministic parsing and linguistic explanation. *Language and Cognitive Processes*, 1:109–134, 1985.
[10] L. Bloomfield. *Language.* Holt, New York, 1933.
[11] P. Bosch. *Agreement and Anaphora: a study of the role of pronouns in syntax and discourse.* Academic Press, London, 1983.
[12] J. F. Canny. *The complexity of robot motion planning.* MIT Press, Cambridge, 1988.
[13] N. Chomsky. The logical structure of linguistic theory. (mimeographed, Harvard. Published in part by Plenum Press, 1975), 1955.
[14] N. Chomsky. Three models for the description of language. *I.R.E. Transations on Information Theory*, IT-2:113–124, 1956. (Reprinted, with corrections, in Luce et. al. 1965).
[15] N. Chomsky. *Aspects of the Theory of Syntax.* MIT Press, Cambridge, 1965.
[16] N. Chomsky. On binding. *Linguistic Inquiry*, 11(1):1–46, 1980.
[17] N. Chomsky. *Rules and Representations.* Columbia University Press, New York, 1980.
[18] N. Chomsky. *Lectures on Government and Binding.* Foris Publications, Dordrecht, 1981.
[19] N. Chomsky. *Barriers.* MIT Press, Cambridge, 1986.
[20] N. Chomsky. *Knowledge of Language: Its Origins, Nature, and Use.* Praeger Publishers, New York, 1986.
[21] N. Chomsky. A personal view. Unpublished ms. presented in Israel, April 1988.
[22] N. Chomsky. Some notes on economy of derivation and representation. In *Functional Heads and Clause Structure*, pages 43–74. MIT Working Papers in Linguistics 10, Cambridge, MA, 1989.
[23] N. Chomsky and M. Halle. *The Sound Pattern of English.* Harper & Row, New York, 1968.
[24] N. Chomsky and G. Miller. Introduction to the formal analysis of natural languages. In R. Luce, R. Bush, and E. Galanter, editors, *Handbook of Mathematical Psychology*, volume II, chapter 11, pages 269–321. John Wiley and Sons, New York, 1963.
[25] G. d. Cordemoy. A philospical discourse concerning speech, conformable to the Cartesian principles, 1667.
[26] F. Cornish. *Anaphoric Relations in English and French.* Croon Helm, London, 1986.
[27] H. E. Dudeney. *536 Puzzles and Curious Problems.* Charles Scribner's Sons, New York, 1967. (Edited with introduction by Martin Gardner).

[28] E. Emmet. *Puzzles for Pleasure*. Emerson Books, New York, 1972.
[29] J. Fodor. *The modularity of mind*. MIT Press, Cambridge, 1983.
[30] K. Fujimura. *The Tokyo Puzzles*. Charles Scribner's Sons, New York, 1978. (ed. by Martin Gardner, trans. by Fumie Adachi).
[31] M. R. Garey and D. S. Johnson. *Computers and Intractability*. W.H. Freeman, New York, 1979.
[32] G. Gazdar. Unbounded dependencies and coordinate structure. *Linguistic Inquiry*, 12:155–184, 1981.
[33] G. Gazdar, E. Klein, G. Pullum, and I. Sag. *Generalized Phrase Structure Grammar*. Basil Blackwell, Oxford, England, 1985.
[34] N. Goodman. On the simplicity of ideas. *Journal of Symbolic Logic*, 8(4):107–121, 1943.
[35] J. Grimshaw. *Argument Structure*. MIT Press, Cambridge, MA, 1990.
[36] K. Hale and J. Keyser. On the syntax of argument structure. Lexicon Project Working Paper 34, MIT Center for Cognitive Science, Cambridge, 1991.
[37] M. Halle and A. Marantz. Distributed morphology and the pieces of inflection. unpublished ms., MIT Department of Linguistics, August 18 1992.
[38] G. Harman. Generative grammars without transformational rules. *Language*, 39:597–616, 1963.
[39] J. Higginbotham. Logical form, binding, and nominals. *Linguistic Inquiry*, 14:395–419, 1983.
[40] J. Higginbotham. On semantics. *Linguistic Inquiry*, 16:547–593, 1985.
[41] J. Higginbotham. Eludications of meaning. *Linguistics and Philosophy*, 12(3):465–517, 1989.
[42] J. Higginbotham. Reference and control. ms., Department of Linguistics, MIT, 1990.
[43] J. Hopcroft and J. Ullman. *Introduction to Automata Theory, Languages, and Computation*. Addison-Wesley, Reading, MA, 1979.
[44] R. Ingria and D. Stallard. A computational mechanism for pronominal reference. In *Proceedings of the 27th Annual Meeting of the Association for Computational Linguistics*, pages 262–271, Vancouver, June 1989.
[45] R. Jackendoff. *Consciousness and the Computational Mind*. MIT Press, Cambridge, MA, 1987.
[46] R. Jackendoff. *Semantic Structures*. MIT Press, Cambridge, MA, 1990.
[47] R. Jakobson and M. Halle. *Fundamentals of Language*. Mouton, The Hague, 1956.
[48] R. M. Karp. Reducibility among combinatorial problems. In R. Miller and J. Thatcher, editors, *Complexity of Computer Computations*, pages 85–103. Plenum Press, New York, 1972.
[49] E. Keenan. Names, quantifiers, and sloppy identity problem. *Papers in Linguistics*, 4(2):211–232, 1971.
[50] P. Kiparsky. Linguistic universals and language change. In E. Bach and R. Harms, editors, *Universals in Linguistic Theory*, pages 171–202. Holt, Reinhart and Winston, New York, 1968.
[51] P. Kiparsky. Explanation in phonology. In S. Peters, editor, *Goals of Linguistic Theory*, pages 189–227. Prentice-Hall, Englewood Cliffs, NJ, 1972.
[52] P. Kiparsky. On the evaluation measure. In A. Bruck, R. Fox, and M. LaGaly, editors, *Papers from the Parasession on Natural Phonology*, pages 328–37. Chicago Linguistic Society, Chicago, IL, 1974.
[53] Y. Kitagawa. Copying identity. *Natural Language and Linguistic Theory*, 9(3):497–536, 1991.
[54] J. Koster. *Domains and Dynasties: the Radical Autonomy of Syntax*. Foris Publications, Dordrecht, 1987.
[55] J. Koster and E. Reuland, editors. *Long-Distance Anaphora*. Cambridge University Press, Cambridge, 1991.

Bibliography

[56] S. Lapointe. *A Theory of Grammatical Agreement*. Outstanding Dissertations in Linguistics. Garland Publishing, New York, 1985.

[57] S. G. Lapointe. Toward a unified theory of agreement. In M. Barlow and C. A. Ferguson, editors, *Agreement in Natural Language: Approaches, Theories, Descriptions*, chapter 4, pages 67–87. CSLI, Stanford, 1988.

[58] S. Lappin and M. McCord. A syntactic filter on pronominal anaphora for slot grammar. In *Proceedings of the 28th Annual Meeting of the Assocation for Computational Linguistics*, pages 135–142, Pittsburgh, June 6–9 1990.

[59] H. Lasnik. Remarks on coreference. *Linguistic Analysis*, 2(1):1–22, 1976.

[60] H. Lasnik. Treatment of disjoint reference. *Journal of Linguistic Research*, 1(4):48–58, 1981.

[61] H. Lasnik. On the necessity of binding conditions. In H. Lasnik, editor, *Essays on Anaphora*, chapter 9, pages 149–167. Kluwer Academic, Dordrecht, 1989.

[62] H. Lasnik and M. Saito. On the nature of proper government. *Linguistic Inquiry*, 15:235–289, 1984.

[63] B. Levin and M. Rappaport. -er nominals: implications for the theory of argument-structure. In E. Wehrli and T. Stowell, editors, *Syntax and the Lexicon*. Academic Press, Orlando, 1989.

[64] D. Lewis. Languages and language. In K. Gunderson, editor, *Mind and Knowledge*. University of Minnesota Press, Minneapolis, 1975.

[65] R. Lieber. *Deconstructing Morphology*. University of Chicago Press, Chicago, 1992.

[66] A. Marantz. *On the Nature of Grammatical Relations*. MIT Press, Cambridge, 1984.

[67] A. Marantz. Asymmetries in double object constructions, 1990. talk at MIT.

[68] M. Marcus. *A Theory of Syntactic Recognition for Natural Language*. MIT Press, Cambridge, 1980.

[69] D. Marr. *Vision*. W.H. Freeman, San Francisco, 1980.

[70] R. May. *Logical Form: Its Structure and Derivation*. MIT Press, Cambridge, 1985.

[71] J. D. McCawley. Meaning and the description of languages. In *Grammar and Meaning*. Taishukan Publishing Co., Tokyo, 1973.

[72] G. Miller and N. Chomsky. Finitary models of language users. In R. Luce, R. Bush, and E. Galanter, editors, *Handbook of Mathematical Psychology*, volume II, chapter 13, pages 419–492. John Wiley and Sons, New York, 1963.

[73] R. Noyer. *Features, Positions, and Affixes in Autonomous Morphological Structure*. PhD thesis, Department of Linguistics and Philosophy, MIT, Cambridge, MA, 1992.

[74] D. M. Pesetsky. *Paths and categories*. PhD thesis, Department of Linguistics and Philosophy, MIT, 1982.

[75] G. Pullum. How many possible human languages are there? *Linguistic Inquiry*, 14(3):447–468, 1983.

[76] G. Pullum. How complex could an agreement system be? In G.Alvarez, B.Brodie, and T.McCoy, editors, *Proceedings of the First Eastern States Conference on Linguistics*, pages 79–103, Columbus, OH, September 28–30 1984. Ohio State University.

[77] J. H. Reif. Complexity of the mover's problem and generalizations. In *Proceedings of the 20th focs*, pages 421–427, New York, 1979. IEEE Computer Society.

[78] J. H. Reif and M. Sharir. Motion planning in the presence of moving obstacles. In *Proceedings of the 26th focs*, pages 144–154, New York, 1985. IEEE Computer Society.

[79] T. Reinhart. *Anaphora and Semantic Interpretation*. The University of Chicago Press, Chicago, 1983.

[80] E. S. Ristad. Linguistic and computational analysis of coordination. Technical report, Department of Electrical Engineering and Computer Science, MIT, Cambridge, MA, May 1985. S.B. thesis.

[81] E. S. Ristad. Sources of complexity in GPSG theory. *Theoretical Linguistics*, 13(1/2):105–124, 1986.

[82] E. S. Ristad. The complexity of human language comprehension. Technical Report 964, Artificial Intelligence Laboratory, MIT, Cambridge, MA, December 1988.

[83] E. S. Ristad. Computational structure of generative phonology and its relation to language comprehension. In *Proceedings of the 28th Annual Meeting of the ACL*, pages 235–242, Pittsburgh, PA, June 6–9 1990.

[84] E. S. Ristad. Computational structure of GPSG models. *Linguistics and Philosophy*, 13(5):523–590, 1990.

[85] E. S. Ristad. *Computational Structure of Human Language*. PhD thesis, Department of Electrical Engineering and Computer Science, MIT, Cambridge, May 1990. (revised version appears as MIT AI Lab TR-1260 and MITWPL dissertation).

[86] E. S. Ristad. Complexity of autosegmental phonology and prosodic morphology. Technical Report 389-92, Department of Computer Science, Princeton University, Princeton, NJ, August 1992.

[87] E. S. Ristad. Complexity of the simplified segmental model. Technical Report 388-92, Department of Computer Science, Princeton University, Princeton, NJ, July 1992.

[88] E. S. Ristad. Morpheme analysis and composition. In E. Ristad, editor, *DIMACS Workshop on Human Language*, pages 29–31, Princeton, NJ, March 20–22 1992.

[89] E. S. Ristad and R. C. Berwick. Computational consequences of agreement and ambiguity in natural language. *Journal of Mathematical Psychology*, 33(4):379–396, 1989.

[90] J. R. Ross. *Constraints on variables in syntax*. PhD thesis, Department of Linguistics and Philosophy, MIT, Cambridge, MA, 1967. (Published in 1986 as *Infinite Syntax!*, Ablex:Norwood NJ).

[91] I. A. Sag. *Deletion and Logical Form*. PhD thesis, Department of Linguistics and Philosophy, MIT, 1976.

[92] E. Sapir. The psychological reality of phonemes. In D. G. Mandelbaum, editor, *Selected Writings of Edward Sapir in Language, Culture and Personality*. University of California Press, Berkeley, 1933. 1949.

[93] P. Sells. Aspects of logophoricity. *Linguistic Inquiry*, 18(3):445–479, 1987.

[94] C. Shannon. A mathematical theory of communication. *Bell System Technical Journal*, 27:379–423, 623–656, 1948.

[95] S. Shieber, S. Stucky, H. Uszkoreit, and J. Robinson. Formal constraints on metarules. In *Proceedings of the 21st Annual Meeting of the ACL*, pages 22–27. Association of Computational Linguistics, 1983.

[96] R. Solomonoff. A formal theory of inductive inference, part i and part ii. *Information and Control*, 7:1–22, 224–254, 1964.

[97] E. P. Stabler, Jr. How are grammars represented? *The Behavioral and Brain Sciences*, 6:391–421, 1983.

[98] L. J. Stockmeyer and A. R. Meyer. Word problems requiring exponential time. In *Proceedings 5th Annual ACM STOC*, pages 1–9, New York, 1973. ACM.

[99] C. Tenny. *Grammaticalizing aspect and affectedness*. PhD thesis, Department of Linguistics and Philosophy, MIT, Cambridge, MA, 1987.

[100] C. Tenny. The aspectual interface hypothesis. Lexicon Project Working Paper 31, MIT Center for Cognitive Science, Cambridge, March 1989.

[101] H. Uszkoreit and S. Peters. Essential variables in metarules. talk presented at the Annual Meeting of the Linguistic Society of America, December 1982.

[102] W. von Humboldt. *Linguistic Variability and Intellectual Development.* Miami Linguistics Series No.9. University of Miami Press, Coral Gables, Florida, 1836. (Translated by George C. Buck and Frithjof A. Raven, 1971).

[103] T. Wasow. *Anaphoric relations in English.* PhD thesis, Department of Linguistics and Philosophy, MIT, 1972. (Published in 1979 as *Anaphora in Generative Grammar*, E. Story–Scientia:Ghent.).

[104] T. Wasow. *Anaphora in Generative Grammar.* E. Story-Scientia Gent, Ghent, 1979.

[105] M. Wax and T. Kailath. Decentralized processing in sensor arrays. *IEEE Trans. ASSP*, 33(4):1123–1129, 1985.

[106] U. Wiesemann, editor. *Pronominal Systems.* Gunter Narr Verlag, Tübingen, 1986.

[107] E. Williams. Discourse and logical form. *Linguistic Inquiry*, 8:101–139, 1977.

[108] E. Williams. The anaphoric nature of θ-roles. *Linguistic Inquiry*, 20(3):425–456, 1989.

[109] E. Williams. Paradigm structures. In E. Ristad, editor, *DIMACS Workshop on Human Language*, page 12, Princeton, NJ, March 20-22 1992.

[110] P. H. Winston. *Artificial Intelligence.* Addison-Wesley, Reading, MA, 2nd edition, 1984.

[111] P. H. Winston. *Artificial Intelligence.* Addison-Wesley, Reading, MA, 3rd edition, 1992.

[112] A. Yao. Computational information theory. In Y. Abu-Mostafa, editor, *Complexity in Information Theory*, pages 1–15. Springer-Verlag, New York, 1988.

Index

$\mathcal{NP}$, 134
$\mathcal{P}$, 134

* annotation, 31

3-CNF, 137
3SAT Problem, 137

Acquisition model, 9
Agreement
    anaphoric, 43
    SAC, 32
Anaphora problem, 21
    analysis of, 28
    complexity of, 35, 46, 64, 88
    in agreement model, 33
    in anaphoric uniqueness model, 45
    in referential dependency model, 49
    incoherent statement of, 23
    statement of, 24
    summary of results, 28
    vs. anaphoric preference problem, 26
    vs. word problems, 27
    with preference function, 26
Anaphoric agreement, 31
    AUC, 43
Anaphoric agreement problem
    complexity of, 35
    statement of, 33
Anaphoric copying problem, 78
Anaphoric element, 21
Anaphoric preference problem
    complexity of, 102
    in copy model, 78
    in function-sharing model, 102
    statement of, 26
    summary of results, 28
    vs. anaphora problem, 26
Anaphoric sharing problem, 102
    complexity of, 102
Anaphoric uniqueness problem
    complexity of, 46
    statement of, 45
Antecedence
    definition of, 22, 32
    extralinguistic, 53n
Asterisk annotation, 31

AUC, 130
    apparent exceptions, 44
    definition of, 43, 98
    extended, 98

Berwick, R., 4n, 116n
Binding conditions, 52
Binding theory, 52, 129
Boolean
    selected literal, 86
Boolean logic, 136, 138
Bosch, P., 33n

C-command, 51
Category
    definition of, 32, 40
    valid, 40
Chomsky, N., 5, 13, 14n, 20, 50, 61n, 75, 118n, 123, 124, 126n, 128n
Chromatic number problem, 136
Circular dependency, 34, 100, 105n
CNF, 137
Coindexing
    vs. subscripts, 22n
Communication, 12
Compatibility, 50
Competence
    vs. performance, 115
Completeness, 135
Complexity thesis
    confidence in, 7
    implications, 15
Composite number problem
    definition of, 133
Comprehension
    model of, 9
    vs. production, 10, 111, 114
Computational complexity
    classes, 134
    introduction to, 133
Computational linguistics, 117
Computational module, 114
Computational problem
    complexity of, 133
    constructive, 133
    decision, 133
    definition of, 133
Computational system, 1, 132

Computational theory of language, 112, 124
Conceptual framework, 9, 110
Control
    object, 56
    subject, 55
Copy model
    statement of, 77
    vs. function-sharing model, 101
Cordemoy's paradox, 110
Coreference
    depiction of, 22
Correctness of RDG, 50
Correspond, 73
Covariant interpretation, 37, 76
    obligatory, 98
    representation of, 97

Decision problem
    definition of, 133
Dependency
    circular, 34, 100, 105
Description language, 125
Deterministic time, 134
Disjoint reference, 49
    depiction of, 22
Dominate
    semantics of, 40

E-language view, 118n
ECM, 53
Edge
    definition of, 136
Ellipsis
    copy model of, 77
    description of, 57
    function-sharing model of, 94
    of VP, 57
    recursive, 75, 96
Emmet, E.R., 27
Extralinguistic information, 9

Factoring problem
    definition of, 133
Feature
    definition of, 32, 40
Finite state machines, 4
Fodor, J., 114
Function-sharing model
    statement of, 94, 101
    vs. copy model, 101

Gazdar, G., 4n
Generative linguistics, 110, 125
GPSG, 4n
Grammar, 118
Graph
    definition of, 135
Graph coloring problem, 136
Grimshaw, J., 25n

Halle, M., 126n
Hardness, 135
Harman, G., 4n
Higginbotham, J., 32, 50, 94n
Human language, 9
Humboldt, W. von, 10n

I-language view, 13, 118n
Immediate antecedence, 22
Incident
    definition of, 136
Inflectional feature system
    definition of, 40
Information encapsulation, 114
Interpretation of language, 9
    constructive, 10
    probabilistic, 11
    submodels, 11
Invariant interpretation, 37, 76
    representation of, 97
Invisible obviation, 57
IOC
    definition of, 59, 63
    explanation of, 96

Jackendoff, R., 25n

Karp, R., 136
Keenan, E., 94n
Kitagawa, Y., 78n, 92n, 93n
Knowledge
    of agreement, 31
    of coreference, 31
    of disjoint reference, 49

Language complexity game
    confidence in, 7
    idea of, 5

Index   147

quiescent state, 8
structure of, 6
Language computation, 1, 10
Language model, 9, 109
Language problems
    vs. mental puzzles, 27
    vs. truth conditions, 27
Lasnik, H., 20, 50
Link
    definition of, 22, 32
    depiction of, 97
Locality, 51
Lower bounds, 7

Marantz, A., 85, 94n
Marcus, M., 4n
Markov models, 4
Marr, D., 110, 116
Miller, G., 123

Nondistinct
    definition of, 32
Novelty Condition, 39

Obviation
    definition of, 49
    depiction of, 97
    invisible, 57
    limits of, 53
Orders of growth, 133

Paradigm structure
    asymmetry in, 99
    definition of, 40, 41
    formalization of, 40
    of English pronouns, 37, 41
    visualization of, 40
    vs. preference function (Υ), 47
Parser, 118
    accuracy of, 119
    correctness of, 118
    efficiency of, 118
Performance
    limits on, 122
    theory of, 121
    vs. competence, 115
Phrase structure tree, 51n
Preference function (Υ)
    complexity of, 26

semantic, 25
vs. paradigm structure, 47
Principles and parameters, 11
PRO
    motivation for, 55
Production
    model of, 9
    vs. comprehension, 10, 111, 114
Pronouns
    agreement properties, 33
PSPACE, 134

QBF Problem, 137

RDG
    compatibility, 50
    correctness of, 50
    definition of, 49
Reduction ($\leq_\mathcal{P}$), 135
Referential dependencies
    complexity of, 88
    graph of, 49
Referential dependencies problem
    complexity of, 64
    statement of, 49
Referential intepretation problem, 21
Referring expression, 21
Reinhart, T., 74
Research program, 2
Robot motion planning, 28
Ross, J.R., 78n

SAC, 130
    complexity of
        A, 36
    critique of, 36
    definition of, 32
    empirical consequences, 36
    empirical problems, 39
Sag, I., 74, 94n
Saito, M., 20
Satisfiability
    of Boolean formulas, 137
Satisfiability Problem (SAT), 137
Selected literal, 86
Semantic role, 25
SPE, 126n
Split antecedence, 34, 50n
Strong crossover, 56
Subscripts

semantics of, $22n$, 97
vs. coindexing, $22n$
Subsume
semantics of, 40
Surface representation, 74

Thematic hierarchy, 25
definition of, $25n$
Trace, 56
Traveling salesman problem
A, 135
Truth assignment, 136
Turing machine
nondeterministic, 134

Underlying representation, 75
Unitary language computation, 9, 109
Universal grammar, 9
Upper bounds, 7

Valid category, 40
Vertex
definition of, 136

Wasow, T., 39
Weinberg, A., $4n$, $116n$
Wh-movement, 56
Williams, E., 40, 74
Word problem, 27
example, $27n$

Artificial Intelligence
Patrick Henry Winston, founding editor
J. Michael Brady, Daniel G. Bobrow, and Randall Davis, current editors

Artificial Intelligence: An MIT Perspective, Volume I: Expert Problem Solving, Natural Language Understanding, Intelligent Computer Coaches, Representation and Learning, edited by Patrick Henry Winston and Richard Henry Brown, 1979

Artificial Intelligence: An MIT Perspective, Volume II: Understanding Vision, Manipulation, Computer Design, Symbol Manipulation, edited by Patrick Henry Winston and Richard Henry Brown, 1979

NETL: A System for Representing and Using Real-World Knowledge, Scott Fahlman, 1979

The Interpretation of Visual Motion, by Shimon Ullman, 1979

A Theory of Syntactic Recognition for Natural Language, Mitchell P. Marcus, 1980

Turtle Geometry: The Computer as a Medium for Exploring Mathematics, Harold Abelson and Andrea di Sessa, 1981

From Images to Surfaces: A Computational Study of the Human Visual System, William Eric Leifur Grimson, 1981

Robot Manipulators: Mathematics, Programming, and Control, Richard P. Paul, 1981

Computational Models of Discourse, edited by Michael Brady and Robert C. Berwick, 1982

Robot Motion: Planning and Control, edited by Michael Brady, John M. Hollerbach, Timothy Johnson, Tomás Lozano-Pérez, and Matthew T. Mason, 1982

In-Depth Understanding: A Computer Model of Integrated Processing for Narrative Comprehension, Michael G. Dyer, 1983

Robotic Research: The First International Symposium, edited by Hideo Hanafusa and Hirochika Inoue, 1985

Robot Hands and the Mechanics of Manipulation, Matthew T. Mason and J. Kenneth Salisbury, Jr., 1985

The Acquisition of Syntactic Knowledge, Robert C. Berwick, 1985

The Connection Machine, W. Daniel Hillis, 1985

Legged Robots that Balance, Marc H. Raibert, 1986

Robotics Research: The Third International Symposium, edited by O.D. Faugeras and Georges Giralt, 1986

Machine Interpretation of Line Drawings, Kokichi Sugihara, 1986

ACTORS: A Model of Concurrent Computation in Distributed Systems, Gul A. Agha, 1986

Knowledge-Based Tutoring: The GUIDON Program, William Clancey, 1987

AI in the 1980s and Beyond: An MIT Survey, edited by W. Eric L. Grimson and Ramesh S. Patil, 1987

Visual Reconstruction, Andrew Blake and Andrew Zisserman, 1987

Reasoning about Change: Time and Causation from the Standpoint of Artificial Intelligence, Yoav Shoham, 1988

Model-Based Control of a Robot Manipulator, Chae H. An, Christopher G. Atkeson, and John M. Hollerbach, 1988

A Robot Ping-Pong Player: Experiment in Real-Time Intelligent Control, Russell L. Andersson, 1988

Robotics Research: The Fourth International Symposium, edited by Robert C. Bolles and Bernard Roth, 1988

The Paralation Model: Architecture-Independent Parallel Programming, Gary Sabot, 1988

Concurrent System for Knowledge Processing: An Actor Perspective, edited by Carl Hewitt and Gul Agha, 1989

Automated Deduction in Nonclassical Logics: Efficient Matrix Proof Methods for Modal and Intuitionistic Logics, Lincoln Wallen, 1989

Shape from Shading, edited by Berthold K.P. Horn and Michael J. Brooks, 1989

Ontic: A Knowledge Representation System for Mathematics, David A. McAllester, 1989

Solid Shape, Jan J. Koenderink, 1990

Expert Systems: Human Issues, edited by Dianne Berry and Anna Hart, 1990

Artificial Intelligence: Concepts and Applications, edited by A. R. Mirzai, 1990

Robotics Research: The Fifth International Symposium, edited by Hirofumi Miura and Suguru Arimoto, 1990

Theories of Comparative Analysis, Daniel S. Weld, 1990

Artificial Intelligence at MIT: Expanding Frontiers, edited by Patrick Henry Winston and Sarah Alexandra Shellard, 1990

Vector Models for Data-Parallel Computing, Guy E. Blelloch, 1990

Experiments in the Machine Interpretation of Visual Motion, David W. Murray and Bernard F. Buxton, 1990

Object Recognition by Computer: The Role of Geometric Constraints, W. Eric L. Grimson, 1990

Representing and Reasoning With Probabilistic Knowledge: A Logical Approach to Probabilities, Fahiem Bacchus, 1990

3D Model Recognition from Stereoscopic Cues, edited by John E.W. Mayhew and John P. Frisby, 1991

Artificial Vision for Mobile Robots: Stereo Vision and Multisensory Perception, Nicholas Ayache, 1991

Truth and Modality for Knowledge Representation, Raymond Turner, 1991

Made-Up Minds: A Constructivist Approach to Artificial Intelligence, Gary L. Drescher, 1991

Vision, Instruction, and Action, David Chapman, 1991

Do the Right Thing: Studies in Limited Rationality, Stuart Russell and Eric Wefeld, 1991

KAM: A System for Intelligently Guiding Numerical Experimentation by Computer, Kenneth Man-Kam Yip, 1991

Solving Geometric Constraint Systems: A Case Study in Kinematics, Glenn A. Kramer, 1992

Geometric Invariants in Computer Vision, edited by Joseph Mundy and Andrew Zisserman, 1992

HANDEY: A Robot Task Planner, Tomás Lozano-Pérez, Joseph L. Jones, Emmanuel Mazer, and Patrick A. O'Donnell, 1992

Active Vision, edited by Andrew Blake and Alan Yuille, 1992

Recent Advances in Qualitative Physics, edited by Boi Faltings and Peter Struss, 1992

Machine Translation: A View from the Lexicon, Bonnie Jean Dorr, 1993

The Language Complexity Game, Eric Sven Ristad, 1993

The MIT Press, with Peter Denning as general consulting editor, publishes computer science books in the following series:

ACL-MIT Press Series in Natural Language Processing
Aravind K. Joshi, Karen Sparck Jones, and Mark Y. Liberman, editors

ACM Doctoral Dissertation Award and Distinguished Dissertation Series

Artificial Intelligence
Patrick Winston, founding editor
J. Michael Brady, Daniel G. Bobrow, and Randall Davis, editors

Charles Babbage Institute Reprint Series for the History of Computing
Martin Campbell-Kelly, editor

Computer Systems
Herb Schwetman, editor

Explorations with Logo
E. Paul Goldenberg, editor

Foundations of Computing
Michael Garey and Albert Meyer, editors

History of Computing
I. Bernard Cohen and William Aspray, editors

Logic Programming
Ehud Shapiro, editor; Fernando Pereira, Koichi Furukawa, Jean-Louis Lassez, and David H. D. Warren, associate editors

The MIT Press Electrical Engineering and Computer Science Series

Research Monographs in Parallel and Distributed Processing
Christopher Jesshope and David Klappholz, editors

Scientific and Engineering Computation
Janusz Kowalik, editor

Technical Communication and Information Systems
Edward Barrett, editor